The Pro
vs.
The Prophet
The Preacher Who Refused To Quit

PAUL
SCHWANKE

First published by Paul Schwanke,
an Independent Baptist evangelist from Phoenix, Arizona.
Evangelist Schwanke is committed to preaching
and providing materials to assist pastors and churches
in the fulfillment of the Great Commission.

Evangelist Paul Schwanke
www.preachthebible.com

Cover design by Mr. Rick Lopez
www.outreachstudio.com

Special thanks to Pastor Ken Brooks
and to Mom Schwanke

ISBN-13: 978-1514345528
ISBN-10: 1514345528

Printed in the United States of America

CONTENTS

THE ONLY THING MISSING was the golden voice of Michael Buffer and his trademark phrase: "Let's get ready to rumble!" Boxing fans testify that the greatest fight of all time was the classic 'Thrilla in Manila,' where Muhammad Ali and Smokin' Joe Frazier warred for fourteen rounds. They had nothing on the 'Battle of Bethel' - the conflict of Amos chapter 7.

"In this corner, wearing the refined robe of the cultured clergy: the sophisticated seminarian, the distinguished doctor, the polished pedagogue, the ingenious intellectual, the "priest of Bethel" himself - Doctor Amaziah!"

The adoring crowd went wild. Sitting in the ringside seats were the princes of the land, the powerful political elite, and King Jeroboam himself. The wealthy businessmen, who had a lot riding on this battle, had come along with their pompous wives all decked out in furs and jewelry. Of course, the members of the Ministerial Association of Bethel, the sponsoring agency for this event, were out in force. In the cheap seats were the lap-dog seminary students of Bethel Reformed Seminary. They had all come to see their hero, Doctor Amaziah, pulverize this irritating meddler once and for all.

"And in this corner, wearing a...sheepskin? Here he is: the humble herdman, the simple sycamore man - Amos of Tekoa!"

It seemed destined to be a one-sided affair. Mike Tyson was famous for winning twelve of his first nineteen professional bouts in the first round. He once won a championship belt by knocking out Michael Spinks in 91 seconds.[1]

No one expected Amos to last 91 seconds with Doctor Amaziah, who was after all, the "priest of Bethel." Worse, this battle was being held at the "king's chapel" which was located in the "king's court" (Amos 7:10, 13). It was the ultimate home field advantage.

Amos must have looked at the multitude and wondered how all this happened. His quiet little hometown of Tekoa, nineteen miles to the south, must have seemed light years away. The erudite highbrows that filled this city of Bethel were polar opposites from the common folk who lived in the rolling hills and the lush valleys of southern Judah. In all of the Bible, it would be hard to find a man more out of his element than Amos was on that day. He had to ask himself, "How did I get here?"

But he was not in that ring by accident. 'How he got there' was orchestrated by a God who wanted people that were too comfortable to know how precarious their days were. 'How he got there' describes in vivid and surprising detail what the judgment of God looks like. 'How he got there' portrays a God who is giving His people one last chance.

'How he got there' is the story of the book of Amos.

Chapter One
The LORD Took Me

IT ALL STARTED simply enough: "The words of Amos, who was among the herdmen of Tekoa" (Amos 1:1). Of the sixteen writing prophets in the Old Testament, Amos was the only one who told us what his occupation was before God called him.[2] He was a shepherd and a "gatherer of sycomore fruit" (Amos 7:14). In order to make ends meet, Amos had to hold down two jobs.

Amos wasn't the owner of the ranch or a wealthy business partner; he was simply a worker that was "among" all of the others. He did not own the sycomores; he gathered them. Tekoa was a poor place where people did whatever was necessary to put food on the table. When the Bible says he gathered sycomore fruit (or figs), he was collecting the food that the poorest of the land would eat. He would then need to scratch open the figs so they would ripen and be edible.

Modern scholars go out of their way to paint a picture of Amos that the Bible does not give. Some have assumed, on the basis of his eloquent style of preaching, that he must have been a world traveler with an extensive education. That is the funny thing about modern scholarship. They are quite certain that a man can only be successful if he obtains one of their degrees and is certified with their stamp of approval. They do not entertain the possibility that a man might actually be taught of God.

Amos never experienced such formal training. He told Dr. Amaziah: "I *was* no prophet, neither *was* I a prophet's son" (Amos 7:14). He never sat in their classrooms to receive instruction. He did not walk the line, flip the tassel, and accept one of their diplomas. He never passed one of their ordination councils, nor was he an official member of the 'Prophets Guild of Bethel.'[3] He was not called by a fellowship, a convention, a presbytery, a seminary, or a missions board. There was no plaque on the wall reminding the world of his accomplishments. When his name was written, there was no ThM, MA, STM, PhD, D.Min, or DTS following it. No one called him Doctor Amos, Professor Amos, or (worse) Reverend Amos.[4]

Do we understand how unwelcome Amos would be in most churches and religious institutions today? We might well imagine a Seminary president sitting before an accreditation commission. The chairman says, "As you well know, the purpose of our agency is to ensure before the US Department of Education that the education you provide 'meets acceptable levels of quality.'[5] We have examined and approve your library. We have examined and approve your financial statements. We have examined and approve your facilities. We have examined and approve your curriculum. All seemed to be in order until we examined your faculty,[6] and there we found a problem. You have this professor named Amos. He is not credentialed. He is not degreed. He does not possess 'high academic quality.' I am afraid we cannot approve Him. Perhaps you have a twenty-four year old graduate assistant with the appropriate qualifications?"

Amos' biography was summed up like this: "And the LORD took me as I followed the flock, and the LORD said unto me, Go, prophesy unto my people Israel" (Amos 7:15). That was the extent of His calling. God took him. God called him. That may not be good enough for the Department of Education, but it is enough to qualify a man to pen Scripture.

It is the difference between the hireling and the man of God. God's man is not called by a school, a board, or a council; he is called by God. He does not preach because that is the source of income; he preaches because one day God "took" him. When Amos was minding his own business in the hill country of southern Judah, God snatched him away from the animals and the sycamores with a call from Heaven. It sounded like this: "Go, prophesy unto my people Israel" (Amos 7:15). He was not employed by the seminary at Bethel; he was commissioned by God.

It is the reason Amaziah had a profoundly difficult time comprehending Amos. In his world, a prophet or priest was doing a job to make money and put bread on the table.

He figured that he had Bethel covered, so he told Amos to "flee thee away into the land of Judah, and there eat bread, and prophesy there" (Amos 7:12). It was all territorial. "I've got the land of Bethel. You take the land of Judah." It never dawned upon him that a prophet of God was not sent to a location. He was sent "unto my people Israel" (Amos 7:15).

A job or a calling - it makes all the difference in the world. Amaziah had risen through the ranks and was now honored with the plum job of vicar in "the king's chapel and...the king's court." It was King Jeroboam himself who established Bethel as one of two religious centers in the kingdom, and it was the king who installed him as "the priest of Bethel" (Amos 7:10). He was not simply *a* priest of Bethel, he was *the* priest of Bethel.

Occasionally liberal ministers accidentally tell the truth. When Amaziah told Amos that Bethel was "the king's chapel and...the king's court," he probably did not understand how accurate that statement was. The king was running the show and the God of the Bible was not welcome. If Amaziah was going to put dinner on the table, he had to make sure he never upset the king. Every word was tempered for the approval of the royals.

Amos had a very different preaching philosophy. He did not answer to a board, a politician, or a fellowship; he answered to God. As such, when he preached, it sounded like this: "The lion hath roared, who will not fear? the Lord GOD hath spoken, who can but prophesy?" (Amos 3:8) Amos did not have a choice. He had to speak because God had spoken.

It is not hard to tell the difference between a man who gets his message from the Bible and the man who gets his message from the internet. Sunday morning quickly separates the man full of God's Word who roars out the words of God, and the man who is doing everything humanly possible to avoid offending anyone.

The late Dr. J. Wilbur Chapman used to tell of an old preacher who often spoke on the subject of sin. He minced no words, but defined it as "that abominable thing that God hates." A leader in his congregation came to him on one occasion and urged him to cease using the word 'ugly.' Said he: "Pastor, we wish you would not speak so plainly about sin. Our young people, hearing you, will be more likely to indulge in sin. Call it something else, as 'inhibition,' or 'error' or a 'mistake,' or even 'a twist in our nature.'"

"I understand what you mean," the preacher remarked as he went to his desk and brought out a little bottle. "This bottle," he said, "contains strychnine. You will see that the red label here reads 'Poison.' Would you suggest that I change the label, and paste one on that says, 'Wintergreen?' The more harmless the name the more dangerous the dose will be."[7]

The kind of preaching that comes out of the mouth of a man depends solely on whom he is trying to please. If he is preaching to please humans, his soothing words will tickle their ears. If he is preaching to please God, he will roar like a lion. It is the difference between a prophet of God and a priest of Bethel. It is the difference between a man taught by God and a man taught by a professor. It is the difference between a preacher and a professional.

It is the difference between an Amos and an Amaziah.

Chapter Two

The Pain in the Neck

THE YEAR WAS 760 BC, and it was a great time to be alive in the land of Israel. King Jereboam was doing an excellent job of expanding the kingdom just as King Uzziah had done down south in Judah, and the peace and cooperation that existed between the two nations was more than unusual. Expanding trade routes meant that business was booming, the 'stock market' was climbing, and people were enjoying their luxurious lifestyles. They were a sophisticated, cultural, proud people.

A real enemy, the Assyrian army, was rising on the world scene, but Israel was not too concerned. They were convinced by their military pundits that their army could protect them, and with the mighty mountains to the east and the Great Mediterranean to the west, there was no reason for alarm.

There was just enough religion for everyone to feel good about themselves. It had been some thirty years since Elisha had preached his final message, and without a prophet of God to upset the apple cart, the business of religion was flourishing. The religious capital, Bethel, was the very place where God met their fathers Abraham and Jacob, yet now a pagan temple stood on these once hallowed grounds.

Little did the people know it was "two years before the earthquake" (Amos 1:1). The Jewish historian, Josephus, claimed the earthquake moved half a mountain. It was so powerful that two hundred years later the prophet Zechariah would remind people of the day they "fled from before the earthquake" (Zechariah 14:5). Recent excavations give evidence of a massive temblor that caused great havoc.[8] That earthquake would not be the only thing that would shake the land. The rising Assyrian army would be a tool of the judgment of God that no one saw coming.

So God raised up Amos. His name means to "be a burden-bearer; one with a burden."[9] The idea is not that Amos had a heavy load that he was carrying in his heart. Rather, the name means that Amos was a heavy load to the people to whom he was preaching. In our day, we might call a preacher like Amos a 'pain in the neck.' Over the centuries there were many men of God from the Northern Kingdom that went south to preach to Judah and Jerusalem. Beginning with Amos, God reversed that process. The 'southerners' would now be preaching to the 'Yankees,' and over the next twenty-five years Hosea, Isaiah, and Micah would follow the path blazed by Amos.

Amos must have been quite the preacher to hear. His words are often poetic and flow with a great rhythm. His illustrations are vivid descriptions of rushing streams, withered fields, damaging locusts, hills dripping with sweet wine, birds caught in traps, and roaring lions. Like an artist, he paints impressive visions of mountain summits, massive citadels, rich pasture land, and flowing rivers.[10] On three occasions, Amos breaks out into singing, combining mighty preaching with glorious music. He must have been a pleasure to hear.

The first section of the book were the "words of Amos" (Amos 1:1). God declared the message this man was to preach and he was faithful to those very words spoken by God. In chapter seven, the method of inspiration changed, and the final three chapters were not simply a man delivering the words of God, but rather a prophet describing five visions of God. In chapter one, he is saying, "This is what God told me." In chapter seven, he is preaching, "This is what God showed me."

He was a man delivering a burden. Little did anyone know, but the nation to whom he was preaching had less than forty years left. Amos was the first in a string of men that would give them their last chance.

Had Amos been able to go to Dr. Amaziah's homiletics class, he would have learned the appropriate way to start a message. He would have been taught to "ease into the message; never be too blunt." He would have learned how to tell a funny joke or a quaint story. But the old country bumpkin didn't have 'much trainin.' All he knew to do was open his mouth and tell the people what God told him, and this is what he said:

"The LORD will roar" (Amos 1:2).

There was a choice to be made. Would they heed the roaring lion known as Amos? Would they be drawn to the dulcet speech of Amaziah?

Chapter Three
The Lion Roars

YOU MAY HAVE HEARD THE STORY ABOUT the man who bragged that he had cut off the tail of a man-eating lion with his pocket knife. Asked why he hadn't cut off the lion's head, he replied: "Someone had already done that."

Years ago, after preaching a meeting in Thika, Kenya, I had the privilege of spending a few nights at a tented camp in the Masai Mara. The multitude of animals and the incredibly beautiful savanna made for the trip of a lifetime. Yet for all the sights, the most memorable event was not seen but heard. Lying in a tent in the middle of a quiet African night, there is nothing quite like the earth shaking roar of a lion. At night the air is thinner and the sound travels farther, and the intense darkness of the jungle makes the sound all the more terrorizing. When the lion roars, the rest of the jungle stops. The king has something to say.

As a sheep-herder in southern Judah, Amos likely had many encounters with lions. Now he was dealing with the

'Lion of the Tribe of Judah,' and the first words out of the mouth of Amos the preacher were these: "The LORD will roar from Zion, and utter his voice from Jerusalem; and the habitations of the shepherds shall mourn, and the top of Carmel shall wither" (Amos 1:2). It took one sentence for Amos to get to his point. Their human religion created at Bethel and Dan did not involve Jehovah God. His voice did not emanate from their houses of worship. His stamp of approval was still on the house of David in Jerusalem.

Imagine the power of the roaring words of God! When He cries out in Jerusalem, the effect is felt 67 miles away on the top of Mount Carmel. Lush "galleries" (Song of Solomon 7:5) of vegetation on the top of the mountain chain instantly dry up at the blast of his voice. The last time a man of God stood on Mount Carmel, the mighty fire of God burned a bull on the rebuilt altar. Now another man of God had come to proclaim, "Thus saith the LORD" (Amos 1:3).

Amos begins by preaching seven messages of judgment against the neighbors of Israel. It is easy to imagine the crowds gathering as this country preacher hammered their enemies. While preaching in local churches, I have discovered there are sins that are popular to preach against. So long as we are dealing with the 'national' sins of America, people like it. When the wicked 'out there' are condemned there are a lot of "amens." But "the time *is come* that judgment must begin at the house of God" (1 Peter 4:17), and when such a message is preached in the church, the 'amens' seem to stop. Amos would ultimately point out to Israel that the problem was not 'out there,' it was 'right here.'

Amos repeatedly used this phrase: "For three transgressions...and for four, I will not turn away *the punishment* thereof." It became the outline for the indictments against the wicked nations. The words were a very poignant way of preaching that by breaking God's law the people had exhausted the patience and the mercy of God. In effect, Amos was saying, "You have sinned and sinned and sinned against the Lord; this is the final sin that has triggered the wrath of God!" It was a powerful way of demonstrating that the sins of these nations were multiplied before the Holy God of the Bible, and the cumulative effect would not be dismissed.

The numerous transgressions had led to the final sin. Amos does not list the sins that led to this point, but he says that each of the seven surrounding nations of Israel had gone so far that God would "not turn away *the punishment.*" It takes a lot for humans to exhaust the One whose "mercy *is* great unto the heavens" (Psalm 57:10).

From Amos 1:3-2:5, the man of God exposes the one major sin of the surrounding nations that triggered the judgment of God. He traverses the points of the compass beginning with Damascus, Syria, to the northeast. Gaza lay to the southwest of Israel, Tyre to the northwest, Edom to the southeast, Ammon to the east, Moab to the southeast, and Judah to the south. No one would escape the holy wrath of God.

Amos started by condemning the cruelty of Damascus, a people that were bitter enemies of his audience. The great grandparents could recall the days when King Hazael had taken their territory and terrorized them. Now God was promising retribution.

Their 'fourth' sin, the straw that 'broke the camel's back,' involved threshing "Gilead with threshing instruments of iron" (Amos 1:3). Conquering enemy cities was not enough for their military; they destroyed villages and massacred people, committing wartime atrocities. As freshly harvested grain was dragged over iron prongs to separate the wheat from the chaff, innocent people were cruelly slaughtered in cold blood. The history books did not record the particular incident of verse three, but God did. These terrorists would answer to Him.

God promised to burn down the "house of Hazael" and eliminate their dynasties (Amos 1:4). The people felt protected if their city gates had a massive iron security bar, but He promised to "break also the bar of Damascus" (Amos 1:5). When their final chapter was written, God said that they would "go into captivity unto Kir." Centuries earlier they had escaped Kir and established their own nation, but the day was coming where they would end up back where they started. God would stamp the word 'futile' as their permanent legacy.

Our world seems to turn a blind eye to similar terrorism. Violent Islamic acts against Christians around the world occasionally are reported, but they are soon forgotten. Cowardly politicians and a politically correct news media refuse to acknowledge the atrocities and hold evil men accountable. God doesn't need an army nor a studio. He will defend the defenseless as the bloodthirsty will meet an enemy they cannot overcome.

To the southwest was Gaza, a critical port city and chief town of the Philistine empire. When Amos added the cities of Ashdod, Ashkelon, and Ekron to the list, he was condemning the entire nation. Their 'fourth' sin was the crime of capturing a small town, carrying "away captive" the citizens, and selling them as slaves to the Edomites (Amos 1:6).

Very few human atrocities have approached the horrors of the slave industry. When preaching in Ghana, West Africa, I once visited the Cape Coast Castle, the home of slave traders. Men and women were brought from warring tribes throughout that region of Africa and chained in tiny holding cells. It became known as the 'gate of no return' for the hundreds of villagers crammed into that room. From there, they would be loaded onto ships where they usually would be carried to the Caribbean and then sold.

It is difficult to believe the depravity of the village warriors that sold their own brothers into bondage, the European lords that merchandised humanity, and the barbaric seamen who cared nothing for life. The hypocrisy of our modern world rightly condemns those acts of centuries past but does little when innocent young girls are herded into slavery by Islamic traders or prostitution rings.

God notices. Be it the Philistines of 2700 years ago or godless pagans today, He makes a promise: "I will not turn away; I will send a fire; I will cut off; I will turn mine hand against" (Amos 1:7-8). When the dust settles, they will "perish."

As impossible as it might seem, the city of Tyre outdid the armies of Gaza. The Bible says they "delivered up the whole captivity to Edom," uprooting entire settlements and communities and selling them into slavery. A long standing "brotherly covenant" (Amos 1:9) made between Solomon and Hiram was broken, leading God to promise that He would "send a fire on the wall of Tyrus...(and) devour the palaces" (Amos 1:10). Walls symbolized the greatest strength of a city and the palace displayed their political power, but both would melt before the wrath of God.

Then God called Edom to step forth. Edom had a history with Israel that went all the way back to the womb of Rebecca where their father Esau wrestled with Jacob. They never settled their family hostility. Through the centuries "he did pursue his brother with the sword, and did cast off all pity, and his anger did tear perpetually, and he kept his wrath for ever" (Amos 1:11). This family feud had carried on for 1100 years worsening through the centuries. "He kept his wrath for ever."

Obadiah preached against Edomite pride that laughed as their own brothers went into judgment: "The pride of thine heart hath deceived thee, thou that dwellest in the clefts of the rock, whose habitation *is* high; that saith in his heart, Who shall bring me down to the ground? Though thou exalt *thyself* as the eagle, and though thou set thy nest among the stars, thence will I bring thee down, saith the LORD" (Obadiah 3-4). God promised to burn their southern city of Teman and to devour the northern city of Bozrah.

The Israelites and the Edomites have a great lesson to teach us today. Family battles will not go quietly away. The bitterness and anger that separated Esau and Jacob became the template for centuries of wars and hatred. They became a Bible version of the Hatfields and the McCoys.

Next, God calls out the sins of the children of Ammon. Their ancestor was conceived by the wicked incestuous relationship between Lot and one of his daughters. At times, the Ammonites and the Israelites fought it out on the battlefield. On other occasions, Satan tempted Israel with the false gods of the Ammonites.

Their Bible describes their 'fourth' sin with these horrifying words: "they have ripped up the women with child of Gilead" (Amos 1:13). Their insatiable desire for more power and wealth led them to murder helpless babies who were still inside their mothers. They were fighting with Gilead and did not want any future soldiers to get in their way.

As they attacked the babies, God promised to send attackers against them. It would be a whirlwind of wrath as their precious cities would be conquered and they would be led out as slaves.

What an indictment against the abortion business today! Murderous doctors and nurses rip out little babies to enlarge their businesses. Cowardly politicians deny unborn children the right to life, liberty, and the pursuit of happiness. Evil judges refuse to protect the most innocent of all. Yet these evil people who callously destroy unborn children will meet a God of terror. They will reap what they have sown.

It should be noted that God is very specific when dealing with the sins of these nations. God does not judge indiscriminately; He judges righteously. In such manner He called out the Moabites for burning "the bones of the king of Edom into lime" (Amos 2:1). It was not enough for Moab to defeat Edom in war; they disgraced Edom. By burning the bones of the king, they were committing an act of desecration that was beyond the point of human respect. Very possibly, the chalky "lime" may have been used as a whitewash.[11]

As they burned the bones of their enemy, God promised to "send a fire upon Moab" (Amos 2:2). The punishment would fit the crime and the conquering enemy would leave them shouting in pain and tumult.

The intense preaching of Amos was bold and plain. The gathering crowd must have listened in stunned shock at such words. Certainly their preferred minister, Doctor Azariah, would never preach such a message. They listened as Amos preached against their brothers in the land of Judah: "they have despised the law of the LORD, and have not kept his commandments, and their lies caused them to err, after the which their fathers have walked" (Amos 2:4).

The greatest sin of God's people in Judah was rejecting the Word of God. They despised the Bible and disobeyed the Bible. When they created their own system of idols and false religion God called it a lie, a lie which caused them to live in error. For their great sin of rejecting God's law and creating their own religion, God promised to burn down the city of Jerusalem.

Notice the list of these 'fourth' sins: Wartime atrocities; threshing the enemy; terrorism; slave trading; ripping children out of the womb; degrading the dead. Now God adds to this list the sin of rejecting the Bible. Not many humans would agree with God. Not the ministers who refuse to preach the Bible. Not the seminary professors who attack the credibility of the Bible. Not the judges who remove the Bible from our society. Not the Hollywood elites who taunt the Bible. Not the average citizen who never reads or considers the Bible.

Some eight centuries would go by before the Son of God would explain why a sin against the Bible is so serious. He said it like this: "He that rejecteth me, and receiveth not my words, hath one that judgeth him: the word that I have spoken, the same shall judge him in the last day" (John 12:48). The minister who refuses to preach the Bible will be condemned to Hell by the Bible. The seminary professor who destroys the faith of an eager young student will be destroyed by the very words he denies. The judges who exalt their human wisdom above God's wisdom will be silenced by The Book. The entertainment industry will discover too late that "God is not mocked." The sinner who never cared enough to open a Bible will realize he is without excuse.

The lion roared. The King had something to say. The nation of Israel was forced to make a choice. They could listen to the priest of Bethel or they could listen to the man of God.

Their choice determined their future.

Chapter Four

Meddlin'

YEARS AGO a woman sat in a revival meeting, soaking up the message. As the preacher blasted the booze industry, she shouted, "Amen!" When he hit the tobacco industry, she cried out, "That is good preaching!" But when he preached against gossip, she turned to her neighbor and said, "He just stopped preachin' and started meddlin'."

It was time for Amos to start meddlin'. Having preached against the sins of all the neighbors, he turned his attention for the rest of the book to the people right in front of him, the nation of Israel. Like the other nations, they reached their 'fourth' sin.

"Thus saith the LORD; For three transgressions of Israel, and for four, I will not turn away the punishment thereof; because they sold the righteous for silver, and the poor for a pair of shoes; That pant after the dust of the earth on the head of the poor, and turn aside the way of the meek: and a man and his father will go in unto the same maid, to profane my holy name: And they lay

themselves down upon clothes laid to pledge by every altar, and they drink the wine of the condemned in the house of their god" (Amos 2:6-8).

How offensive the preaching of Amos must have been to the people of Bethel! With the statement "for three transgressions of Israel, and for four," the man of God was saying that Israel was no different than the pagan nations surrounding them. They frequently demonstrated an attitude of superiority, taking God for granted, but He would not grant them a national exemption. As He held other nations accountable, so He would demand righteousness from His own people.

The great sin of Israel was their abuse of power which was demonstrated by numerous illustrations. When a poor man needed a loan, a creditor would demand exorbitant interest. If the payment was not made, the loan shark would sell the individual into slavery. They may have owed a debt that was equal to a pair of shoes, but there was no mercy from the ruthless 'Shylock.'

The Bible says the "way of the meek" was turned aside; poor men had no recourse in the courtrooms of the day. When he would plead for justice, the judge would dismiss the case with a wave of the hand. There was no help from those assigned by God to protect the humble.

Their exploitation of the poor included sexual abuse. Maids were humbled by both fathers and sons who taunted and profaned the holy name of God.

They were also violating the Word of God. If a poor man was heavily fined in the courts, he might leave his coat behind as bail. When he left to try and find some money, the wealthy religious phony would use the poor man's coat to stay warm. He didn't care if the man shivered through the night. He didn't care that God said, "If thou at all take thy neighbour's raiment to pledge, thou shalt deliver it unto him by that the sun goeth down" (Exodus 22:26). When those fines were finally paid, the extorted money would be used to buy booze for a party in the house of pagan gods.

It is evil when sin runs rampant in the land, yet the crime is far worse when it is found in the house of religion. God expected the priests to hold a standard of righteousness and demonstrate justice, yet the leaders were the worse criminals. They were not moved when God reminded them that He had previously "destroyed" their enemies, saved them "from the land of Egypt," protected them for "forty years through the wilderness," gave them the "land of the Amorite," and "raised up of your sons for prophets" (Amos 2:9-11). Instead, they turned the preachers into drunks and commanded them, "Prophesy not!"

The temperature was rising. As these verses unfold we can almost feel the holy anger shaking the body of Amos. We can hear the passionate words streaming from his heart. The case is being built before their eyes and God's wrath is being aroused. "Behold, I am pressed under you, as a cart is pressed *that is* full of sheaves" (Amos 1:13). Like an overloaded cart crunching the axles below, the rebellion of Israel has brought the mighty God of the Bible to the place where something must be done.

"Therefore the flight shall perish from the swift, and the strong shall not strengthen his force, neither shall the mighty deliver himself: Neither shall he stand that handleth the bow; and he that is swift of foot shall not deliver himself: neither shall he that rideth the horse deliver himself. And he that is courageous among the mighty shall flee away naked in that day, saith the LORD" (Amos 2:14-16).

The fastest runner will not outrun the judgment of God. The strongest weightlifter will not have the power to set himself free. The greatest archer will not hit the target. The champion jockey will not ride the horse faster than the wrath of Heaven. The most courageous soldier won't even take time to dress when he is running for his life.

Perhaps we don't have enough 'Amoses' that are willing to do some 'meddlin.' It was an easy thing for Amos to condemn the surrounding nations, but when he turned the pulpit 180 degrees and preached to the choir, he was going to get a reaction. Yet his point cannot be missed. God was preparing to deal with Israel for their unrighteousness. The judgment clock was nearing midnight and it was the responsibility of the man of God to clearly detail the reasons.

The mighty Baptist preacher of a past generation, Charles Haddon Spurgeon, put it like this:

Let not modern squeamishness prevent plain speaking concerning everlasting torment. Are we to be more gentle than the apostles? Shall we be wiser than the inspired preachers of the word? Until we feel our minds overshadowed with the dread thought of the sinner's doom we are not in a fit frame for preaching to the unconverted. We shall never persuade men if we are afraid to speak of the judgment and the condemnation of the unrighteous. None so infinitely gracious as our Lord Jesus Christ, yet no preacher ever uttered more faithful words of thunder than he did. It was he who spoke of the place "where their worm dieth not and their fire is not quenched." It was he who said, "These shall go away into everlasting punishment." It was he who spake the parable concerning that man in hell who longed for a drop of water to cool his tongue. We must be as plain as Christ was, as downright in honesty to the souls of men, or we may be called to account for our treachery at the last. If we flatter our fellows into fond dreams as to the littleness of future punishment, they will eternally detest us for so deluding them, and in the world of woe they will invoke perpetual curses upon us for having prophesied smooth things, and having withheld from them the awful truth.[12]

When the anger of God is kindled, we do not need positive preaching, promise preaching, or polite preaching. We need a man willing to do some meddlin'.

Israel had the options laid out before them. On one hand, Doctor Amaziah was worried about the reputation of the "king's chapel" and the "king's court." On the other hand, Amos was worried about the sins destroying the land. Amaziah was offended and indignant; Amos decided to do some meddlin'.

For at the end of the day, the last thing we want is God meddlin' with us.

Chapter Five

"Except They Be Agreed"

WINSTON CHURCHILL, his wary eye fixed on Hitler, was a lone voice in the years preceding World War II. He continually warned his nation and the world of the impending disasters about to befall Europe, but few listened. In 1936, he embarked on a strenuous campaign to awaken England with his cries of alarm. In one article, published in the most prominent newspapers of fourteen countries, he warned that the peoples of Europe were "chattering, busy, sporting, toiling, amused from day to day by headlines and from night to night by cinemas, slipping, sinking, rolling backward to the age when the earth was void and darkness moved upon the face of the waters."

Surely, he argued, it was worth a supreme effort...to control the hideous drift of events and arrest calamity on the threshold. He cried out, "Stop it! Stop it! Stop it!!! NOW is the appointed time."

But few listened.[13]

Amos would have understood Mr. Churchill's burden. A voice crying out for God's truth is pretty much a "voice of one crying in the wilderness" (Luke 3:4). It is the reason that a man who determines to preach the Word must resign himself to the fact that such a walk is a very lonely walk. Men like Amos and Micaiah and Ezekiel and Elijah did not have a lot of friends. It is by design.

Amos was willing to present a question that Israel refused to hear, a question that very few Christians today are willing to consider because it pierces the heart of compromised Christianity. "Can two walk together, except they be agreed?" (Amos 3:3)

A modern Christian walks into a mega-church. They are convinced that a local church exists to minister to their needs. They want a church that plays music that they like and provides a comfortable atmosphere where sin is not exposed. They expect a minister to give them a positive, happy message that will make them laugh, maybe make them cry, but will never convict them.

The minister obliges: "As you take your life's journey, wouldn't you like the Lord to walk along with you? Let him walk by your side so that you can fulfill your destiny."[14] Church members are convinced they can invite God along for the ride as the co-pilot. This arrangement won't do.

One of the mightiest prophets in the Bible was also one of the earliest, a man named Enoch. The Word of God twice describes his life with these words: "And Enoch walked with God" (Genesis 5:22, 24). Notice that the Bible does not say, "And God walked with Enoch." Instead,

Enoch made the choice to walk with God. He would live according to God's laws. He would seek to complete God's will for his life. He would preach God's message to the people. God lays out the rules.

Amos understood. He told the people that they could not walk with God unless it was on His terms. They could not live a half-hearted life. They could not pick and choose which parts of the Bible they would believe. The could not select which sins they would condemn and which sins they would excuse. They could not walk with Him unless they were in agreement with Him and His word. They were not going to meet God half-way.

The preaching of Amos sounds like the warnings of Prime Minister Churchill. The preacher paints vivid pictures of impending disasters. The lion in a dark, thick forest is ready to pounce on its prey. A young cub in a den is defending a fresh kill. The trap in the woods has snapped on its victim. The long blast of the trumpet sounds the alarm of war. Listening to Amos, one can almost feel the hot breath of the lion and hear the shrieking wail of the horn. Disaster is imminent.

Amos chapter 3 has an unmistakeable theme to it. Amos wanted the people to know who was responsible for the impending doom:

> *"Hear this word that the LORD hath spoken against you,*
> *O children of Israel"*
> *I will punish you for all your iniquities"*
> *"Shall there be evil in a city,*
> *and the LORD hath not done it?" (Amos 3:1-2,6)*

The modern-day minister tells people, "God will never do anything to us; He only does things for us." That is not how Amos preached. He had a compulsion from God that forced him to declare truth. "Surely the Lord GOD will do nothing, but he revealeth his secret unto his servants the prophets. The lion hath roared, who will not fear? the Lord GOD hath spoken, who can but prophesy?" (Amos 3:7-8) It is of note that the word "secret" is used in verse 7 and not the word 'secrets'. All of the Bible is the revealed word of God, and it is the responsibility of His man to "declare...all the counsel of God" (Acts 20:27). Selective sermons do not please God.

Legal procedures required two witnesses in a capital case,[15] a necessity as the end result of this trial would bring a death sentence to the nation. These witnesses came from Ashdod and Egypt to the assembly on the mountains of Samaria. Such a notion would have offended the elites to whom Amos preached, for they believed themselves morally superior to the Philistines (people of Ashdod) and the Egyptians.[16]

These witnesses, however, would not take the stand. They were simply there to observe what God was going to do. Five times in chapter three, Amos reminds them that God is doing all the talking. The phrase is "saith the Lord," a statement made a total of 43 times in the book of Amos.

The God of the Bible presents two charges against the people:

First, He said "they know not to do right" (Amos 3:10). They had completely rejected the Word of God given to Moses and the prophets that followed him until they had come to the place where they were ignorant of God's Word. Like many religious people today, they thought they knew the Bible and they thought they knew right from wrong, but their foundation was faulty.

The second indictment said they were storing up "violence and robbery in their palaces." The phrase is a common one in the Old Testament.[17] It described a nation where greed dominated every aspect of society from the king's throne in the palace to the common man in the street. Such greed led to the violation of the poor frequently described in Amos.

The preacher went on to describe the judgment of God in horrific, macabre language: "As the shepherd taketh out of the mouth of the lion two legs, or a piece of an ear; so shall the children of Israel be taken out that dwell in Samaria in the corner of a bed, and in Damascus *in* a couch" (Amos 3:12). When a shepherd lost an animal to a wild beast, he took a small piece of the animal back to the owner to prove his story. Israel's destruction would be so gruesome that body parts would be the final confirmation of the wrath of God.

The punishment would include the "horns of the altar" in Bethel (Amos 3:14). When a fugitive was running for his life and seeking asylum, he could charge into the temple and grab the horns of the altar. It was the last hope for refuge.[18] That last chance would vanish when God's judgment visited the land.

The rich people had a house for the winter and a house for the summer. They were opulent "great houses" made out of ivory (Amos 3:15). Archaeologists have discovered these very houses filled with "beautiful inlaid ivories and other marks of prosperity,"[19] but when God dealt with them, their riches could not save them.

What a contrast! The people could choose between the somber warnings of Amos or the pleasant meditations of Amaziah. Either their wealth had turned them from God or it was the blessing of God. God was either doing something 'to' them or He was doing something 'for' them. They were angering God or they were pleasing God.

It was Amos vs. Amaziah. The prophet vs. the professional minister. Time was running out. The people had a choice to make.

Chapter Six

"Prepare To Meet Thy God"

WHEN WAS THE LAST TIME you heard a song about Hell?

It would be impossible to calculate the number of praise choruses that have been written, but how many songs of judgment are out there? A google search will display songs about Hell, but you won't hear them in church on Sunday. They are composed and performed by Satanic rock groups. Then again, you might hear them in some churches.

Do we realize that David would not be welcome to sing in most modern churches? His philosophy of music stated, "I will sing of mercy and judgment" (Psalm 101:1). 'Feel-good' churches naturally perform 'feel-good' music, and a song that exalts the wrath of God, the judgment of God, or the anger of God is usually not on the playlist for these praise teams.

In Amos 4:12-13, the man of God sings a hymn.[20] Imagine Amos accepting an invitation to a modern church. He is being asked to sing. "Bless our hearts Brother Amos.

Praise Him!" The orchestra plays the introduction, and Amos begins to sing:

"Therefore thus will I do unto thee, O Israel: and because I will do this unto thee, prepare to meet thy God, O Israel. For, lo, he that formeth the mountains, and createth the wind, and declareth unto man what is his thought, that maketh the morning darkness, and treadeth upon the high places of the earth, The LORD, The God of hosts, is his name."

I can imagine the crowd listening to Amos sing that God was going to do something "unto" them. They might guess that *"Something Good is Going to Happen to You,"* but that was not the case. Amos sang that God was going to overthrow *"some* of you, as God overthrew Sodom and Gomorrah" (Amos 4:11). The last verse of the song told them it was now time to "prepare to meet thy God." They were going to have an 'encounter with God,' yet it wasn't going to be such a happy occasion.

The word 'prepare' paints a powerful picture. The Hebrew word means "to set up, to make firm, to establish, to prepare."[21] Amos wanted the people to sit up and take notice, for the day was fast approaching when they would have to give an account of their lives. He then went on to describe the God who would judge them.

He is a powerful judge who formed "the mountains." Amos, it seemed, loved the mountains. The people of Israel often looked to mountains to illustrate the great power of God and joined their father David who said, "Which by his strength setteth fast the mountains; *being* girded with power" (Psalm 65:6). The preacher wanted them to look at a tall mountain and imagine standing before the God who formed it.

The judge created "the wind." One can hear Amos preach, "Imagine a fearful, swirling wind storm. As you are surrounded in the storm with no where to run, you will be overwhelmed by the furious wrath of God!"

Their God declared to them His mind and heart. Many a prophet had invested his life in helping people know the thoughts and intents of God. The many opportunities extended to them meant that much would be "required" of them. (Luke 12:48)

Little did they know that God was turning their "morning (into) darkness." He would soon tread on the "high places" which often housed pagan deities and their vile houses of religion. They were about to see a side of Jehovah God they had never imagined, for He was coming as the "God of hosts" or the God of the armies. He was coming to battle, but the enemy was not a foreign land. God was coming against His people.

Most likely, you will not hear that song on Sunday.

Yet, even in a chapter describing the rising armies of God, there is a testimony of His patience. His intent was not to judge them: His desire was that they would return to Him. God is never indiscriminate in His wrath. He always finds a way to separate a Noah and a Lot from the storm. From Amos 4:6-11, there are no less than eight times that God uses the words "I have." Five more times, the statements are reinforced with the reminder of "saith the LORD." These events were not accidents of nature. They were actions intended to demonstrate the seriousness of their sins.

First, God gave them "cleanness of teeth in all your cities, and want of bread in all your places" (Amos 4:6), a very descriptive statement of a famine in the land. One might expect that hungry stomachs would cause a man to seek the Lord, but they did not repent.

Then God sent them a drought. "I have withholden the rain from you, when *there were* yet three months to the harvest: and I caused it to rain upon one city, and caused it not to rain upon another city: one piece was rained upon, and the piece whereupon it rained not withered. So two *or* three cities wandered unto one city, to drink water; but they were not satisfied: yet have ye not returned unto me, saith the LORD" (Amos 4:7-8). The drought came in the month of March, which was the worst case scenario. The lack of rain would ruin their harvest. To prove it was His judgment, God sent rain upon one city but not its neighbor. The weatherman would have no explanation.

When the drought didn't work, God sent "blasting... mildew...(and) palmerworms." The searing blast of hot desert air dried out their crops making them easy targets for parasites. Their harvest was ruined and their economy in trouble, but their pride kept them from humbling themselves.

The rising death toll from plagues and battles took its toll on their best "young men." The stench of death was a horrible reminder of their rebellion against God, but they were not interested in responding. When some of their cities were overthrown, it was still not enough to get their attention.

So there was nothing left for God to say except these words: "Prepare to meet thy God, O Israel." He had loved them, warned them, and chastened them, but they were immune to it all. They would have to answer for their sins.

There is a great warning for us in these verses. As humans, we have a dangerous tendency to ignore the warnings of God. When things go wrong, we are quick to claim in self-righteousness that we are in the midst of a 'great trial.' It is true that God allows trials and tests to strengthen His people and draw them closer to Him. "That the trial of your faith, being much more precious than of gold that perisheth, though it be tried with fire, might be found unto praise and honour and glory at the appearing of Jesus Christ" (1 Peter 1:7). But it is also true "whom the Lord loveth he chasteneth, and scourgeth every son whom he receiveth" (Hebrews 12:6). A Christian harboring sin in his heart is not in the place where God will test him; he is in the place where God must chasten him.

That was the problem of Amos 4. God was unable to get their attention. When the famine was sore in the land, no doubt their version of Joel Osteen told them, "You have to take the limits off of God."[22] When there was drought, their favorite Joyce Meyer must have said, "Don't panic! This is only a test!"[23] When there were dead bodies everywhere, I suspect their favorite singers were reminding them that "God would never give you more than you can handle."

What is God to do? The chastening hand gets stronger and heavier until there is nothing left but sadly to say, "Prepare to meet thy God." If we will not allow God to deal with us through correction we can only expect Him to find another way. "There is a sin unto death" (1 John 5:16) is the warning from Pastor John. From Paul it sounded like this: "For this cause many *are* weak and sickly among you, and many sleep" (1 Corinthians 11:30).

"Prepare to meet thy God." There once was a day when fearless men stepped into God's pulpits and warned people they would not live forever. There once was a day when mighty men of God preached about a Hell that was real with burning fire and brimstone. There once was a day when people trembled under the conviction of the Holy Spirit of God, fearful they would be cast into the Lake of Fire.

"Prepare to meet thy God." A man who preaches such a message should expect to end up where Amos did - in the heat of the battle. A man who preaches like Amos should never expect to win a popularity contest. A man who preaches such a message should plan on being a lonely man.

It is a message that cannot escape the heart of an Amos. It is a message you will not hear from the tongue of an Amaziah. It is the reason some churches are replete with people that fear God and other churches have a form of religion where people are happy to entertain God for sixty minutes a week. Where are the preachers that will lift up their voice and warn the sinner, *"Prepare to meet thy God!"*

An Arizona resort operator, David Pizer, has a different view of preparing for the future. Like some 1,000 other members of the "cryonics" movement, he has made arrangements to have his body frozen in liquid nitrogen as soon as possible after he dies. In this way, Mr. Pizer, a heavy-set, philosophical man who is 64 years old, hopes to be revived sometime in the future when medicine has advanced far beyond where it stands today. And because Mr. Pizer doesn't wish to return a pauper, he's taken an additional step: He's left his money to himself. With the help of an estate planner, Mr. Pizer has created legal arrangements for a financial trust that will manage his roughly $10 million in land and stock holdings until he is re-animated. Mr. Pizer says that with his money earning interest while he is frozen, he could wake up in 100 years the "richest man in the world."[24]

The man would do well to heed these words: ***Prepare to meet thy God.***

Chapter Seven

The Funeral of a Nation

ED CARTER was a sophomore offensive tackle on the Marshall University Thundering Herd football team in 1969. While the team was preparing to travel to Greenville, North Carolina, to play East Carolina University, Ed received a phone call from his mother informing him that his father had died. Ed went home to Texas for the funeral.

There was still time to get back for the game, but Ed's mother begged him not to go because she thought the plane would crash. Ed obeyed his mother.

On November 14, 1970 the plane carrying the football team and staff crashed leaving 75 dead. There were no survivors. Ed's mother received repeated calls with condolences, but Ed was not on the plane. For the next few weeks, Ed went to numerous funerals of his teammates knowing that God had rescued him for a purpose. Soon he heard the Gospel story, was saved, and is now a preacher.

Ed Carter knows what it is like to go to your own funeral.[25]

Amos had a similar experience. God was taking him to the funeral of his own nation. "Hear ye this word which I take up against you, *even* a lamentation, O house of Israel" (Amos 5:1).

What a striking difference between the last verse of chapter four and the first verse of chapter five. Last heard, Amos was singing a glorious hymn exalting the power of God. He is still singing in chapter 5, but the music has changed from a hymn to a lamentation. The stylistic diversion must have been staggering.

A lamentation was sung at a funeral. During the procession the mourners would chant a "dirge" remembering the deceased and the circumstances of the death.[26] It was a song that would be accompanied by sobs and wailing. In this case, it was sung for the "house of Israel," the entire nation.

The mournful wail starts with these words: "The virgin of Israel is fallen; she shall no more rise: she is forsaken upon her land; *there is* none to raise her up. For thus saith the Lord GOD; The city that went out *by* a thousand shall leave an hundred, and that which went forth *by* an hundred shall leave ten, to the house of Israel" (Amos 5:2-3).

Note the words "is fallen." The chapter takes on an eerie tone as if the prophet has been transported into the future and is witnessing the end of a nation that was still very much in existence. The judgment of God they despised and ridiculed was very real, and to God, it was so certain it may as well have happened already.

Israel would die as a young "virgin." She would be cut down in the prime of life; a nation too young to die. When this relatively youthful nation died, God promised she would never rise again. She would not be able to pull herself up and there would be no other nation strong enough to raise her up. She would die and stay that way. When the mighty Assyrian army conquered her 40 short years later, the nation that once boasted armies of thousands was reduced to but a fraction of its former strength. They were wiped out.

Yet it didn't have to be so. Even with the final blow of God's judgment rising on the horizon, the man of God was sent to deliver the invitation from Heaven. "Seek ye me, and ye shall live" (Amos 5:4).

It truly is amazing to see the simplicity of God's invitations. On the one hand, the Word of God is so profound and so deep that only God could have written it. There are places where the water of the Word is so deep no human has ever discovered how deep it actually goes. But when it comes to a human being rescued from the wrath to come, the Bible suddenly goes to the level of a child.

Such is the message of the shepherd from Tekoa. "Seek ye me, and ye shall live." There was an answer and anyone could hear it, understand it, and obey it. It was as simple as seeking the Lord and only Him. He was not a part of their salvation, He was their only Savior. The promise to them is like the promise we have today. "Believe on the Lord Jesus Christ, and thou shalt be saved" (Acts 16:31).

"Ye shall live." "Shalt be saved." There is no wiggle room when it comes to God's promise. He guaranteed His salvation only if they would seek Him, just as he guarantees His salvation only to those who trust Christ.

Amos went on. He told them, "But seek not Bethel" (Amos 5:5). Bethel was their preeminent house of religion, but God would not be found there. Humans are convinced they need religion and all its trappings if they would find God, but they are looking in the wrong place. They will never find the answer in cathedrals and sacraments and confessionals and services.

"Seek the LORD, and ye shall live; lest he break out like fire in the house of Joseph, and devour *it*, and *there be* none to quench *it* in Bethel" (Amos 5:6). The offer of God always has a deadline. If they did not respond and do so quickly, they would discover that the fire of God's wrath would blaze so that no one could put it out. "Boast not thyself of to morrow; for thou knowest not what a day may bring forth" (Proverbs 27:1).

"*Seek him* that maketh the seven stars and Orion, and turneth the shadow of death into the morning, and maketh the day dark with night: that calleth for the waters of the sea, and poureth them out upon the face of the earth: The LORD *is* his name" (Amos 5:8). In a stunning development, Israel had chosen to follow their pagan astrologers and worship the stars. They were carrying the "tabernacle of your Moloch and Chiun your images, the star of your god, which ye made to yourselves" (Amos 5:26). One can hear Amos preach, "Instead of worshipping the stars, you should be worshipping the One who made the stars."

One more time Amos reminded them. "Seek good, and not evil, that ye may live" (Amos 5:14). Like a loving pastor inviting the sinner to Christ, the patient preacher extended the invitation yet one more time. It is so simple and clear, yet there was a competing voice. Doctor Amaziah and the seminary professors from Bethel were on the warpath telling people to trust their king, their military, and the "mountain of Samaria" (Amos 6:1).

Would they believe Amos or Amaziah?

Chapter Eight

Making Enemies

THERE IS A REASON most families do not discuss politics
or religion. There is no faster way to ruin a gathering than
for someone to get up on a soapbox. So when it comes to
these topics, silence is golden.

It would seem most ministers have an occupational
courtesy that prohibits them from condemning another
religion. As they do not question another 'faith,' they
become indignant when others question their teaching.

Amos never read that ethics book.

The country preacher saved his mightiest punches to
attack the false religion that permeated Israel. From the
moment God told Moses on Mount Sinai, "Thou shalt have
no other gods before me" (Exodus 20:3), the greatest issue
for Israel in the Old Testament became the God or gods
they would serve. The sin that would ultimately doom
them would be the creation of false religion and then
bowing down to the respective idols they had made with
their hands. "I *am* the LORD: that *is* my name: and my

glory will I not give to another, neither my praise to graven images" (Isaiah 42:8).

Amos never shied away from the battle. When it finally culminated in chapter seven, he knew that his uncompromising message had fueled the fire. Had he ignored the religious apostasy and preached a positive message, his life would have been a lot more comfortable. But God does not call a preacher to a comfortable life.

The first salvo was found in chapter four. Amos uses a form of preaching that was never taught in Dr. Amaziah's seminary class. It is a method of preaching that is not found in today's modern homiletics classes. In fact, should a young preacher employ the method of Amos, he would be in danger of flunking out of school.

Amos was brutally sarcastic.

"Hear this word, ye kine of Bashan, that are in the mountain of Samaria, which oppress the poor, which crush the needy, which say to their masters, Bring, and let us drink. The Lord GOD hath sworn by his holiness, that, lo, the days shall come upon you, that he will take you away with hooks, and your posterity with fishhooks. And ye shall go out at the breaches, every cow at that which is before her; and ye shall cast them into the palace, saith the LORD" (Amos 4:1-3).

Imagine a stylish minister standing behind his glass lectern, flashing a toothy Sunday morning smile, and opening his talk with these words: "You ladies are a bunch of cows."

Welcome to the 'Amos School of Homiletics.'

The "kine" were animals from the lush Bashan Valley that were renowned for being fat and well-fed. Amos compared them to the elitist women of Samaria who lived luxurious lifestyles. They were obnoxious oppressors of the poor and needy, building their empires by crushing those who could not defend themselves. These entitled wives expected the world to cater them, demanding that their husbands bring them their food and drink. These 'cows' did not spend much time in the kitchen.

God told His man to be very blunt with these beasts. He said the day was coming when rings would be placed in their noses and they would be led away, hooked as captives. They would line up single file, walk out a hole in the wall made by a battering ram, and spend the rest of their lives as slaves to a king in a distant palace. They spent their lives abusing the poor. Now they would find out how the other half lived.

When Amos finished preaching to the cows, he turned his attention to the ministers. The 'sarcasm meter' is off the charts now:

"Come to Bethel, and transgress; at Gilgal multiply transgression; and bring your sacrifices every morning, and your tithes after three years: And offer a sacrifice of thanksgiving with leaven, and proclaim and publish the free offerings: for this liketh you, O ye children of Israel, saith the Lord GOD" (Amos 4:4-5).

Perhaps Amos spoke the words with a tinge of 'ministerial vibrato' - the phony, deep sounding voice that ministers like to make when they are performing their duties. The ministers would often invite people to shrines at Bethel and Gilgal where they would not only experience a wonderful time of spiritual enrichment, but could also keep the coffers full with their offerings. Bethel, after all, had a rich history with their father Abraham, and Gilgal was their first camp when entering the Promised Land.

Amos mimics them. He tells them to "come," but be sure to bring along their sin. If they were going to live wickedly back home, there was no reason to play the game of the hypocrite just because they were on a religious pilgrimage. They were scrupulous to keep the finer points of law which required a daily sacrifice and a three year tithe,[27] but it was all a show. They loved to "proclaim and publish" what they gave, and when they were honored for their generous gifts to the Lord, they "like(d)" it. They would give only so long as they could be seen.

How dangerous religion is! It will convince a man that he is right with God when he is not. It will teach him that an outward act of devotion can replace a heart that is right with God. It will convince him that he can buy righteous standing with God. It will turn him into hypocrite who has to be seen by men and applauded for his efforts.

So Amos takes a hammer to the religion of Israel, and at the same time, he exposes the business of religion that dominates our society today.

Religion loves places. Bethel, Gilgal, and Beersheba were holy sites to the Israelites. Bethel means "the house of God,"[28] and a trip to such a spot would 'connect' the pilgrim with Father Abraham and Father Jacob. Abraham built his altars there and Jacob's famous dream transpired there, so such a journey would put a man where God was supposed to be. Little did it matter to them that their pagan king had set up a golden calf in Bethel and led the nation down the path of idolatry. The religious experience was the main thing. No wonder God told them, "Bethel shall come to nought" (Amos 5:5). One day it will pass away to nothing, and indeed, it was already nothing in the eyes of God.

Seven miles away at Gilgal, one could visit the monuments erected to commemorate the crossing of the Jordan River. It was at Gilgal the fruits and vegetables of the Land of Promise replaced the daily manna from Heaven. Gilgal was the ultimate symbol of freedom to them, yet God promised, "Gilgal shall surely go into captivity" (Amos 5:5).

Some would make the 52 mile trek from Bethel to Beersheba, where God spoke to Abraham, Isaac, and Jacob. Perhaps their hearts would receive a message from Heaven as well, yet God told them not to waste their time. "Pass not to Beersheba" (Amos 5:5).

2775 years later, things have not changed. People are welcomed to visit Israel so they can have the 'religious experience of a lifetime.' They can dip in the Jordan River like Jesus did; cruise the Sea of Galilee like Peter; see where Jesus was born in Bethlehem. Of course, at every stop, religion has built its cathedral or mosque where people pay a fee to be blessed.

God had a message for Israel and a message for us. He said, "Seek not Bethel." Instead of seeking a place, they should have been looking for the God of Bethel. People don't need a pilgrimage, they need a relationship with God. They need to be born again.

Religion exalts good works. Like many today, the Israelites were convinced their works would impress God. So they brought their "sacrifices every morning...(their) tithes after three years...(they offered) a sacrifice of thanksgiving with leaven, and proclaim(ed) *and* publish(ed) the free offerings." And they liked what they were doing. Their religious works gave them an inner satisfaction that they were impressing God and earning their way to Heaven.

It is the most damning attribute of religion. People are always told the 'do's and the don'ts,' and hopefully, the good will outweigh the bad. As religions change, the definitions of good and bad may differ, but the end result is always the same: a man trying to work his way to Heaven. Ephesian 2:9 makes it clear: "Not of works, lest any man should boast." It is impossible for religion to co-exist with this verse.

Religion minimizes sin. Notice again their pious acts in Amos 4:5: "offer a sacrifice of thanksgiving with leaven, and proclaim *and* publish the free offerings." It is noted that they brought thanksgiving offerings and freewill offerings, but there is no account of their bringing sin offerings to God. Evidently, they did not consider themselves to be so evil.

Unless they repented, God would not accept their offerings. "Though ye offer me burnt offerings and your meat offerings, I will not accept *them*: neither will I regard the peace offerings of your fat beasts" (Amos 5:22). God will not be bought off by a gift. A Catholic indulgence will not buy favor with God, and a 'Faith Promise Missions Offering' in a Baptist church will not excuse sin. God's forgiveness is not for sale.

Religion complicates. How simple is the message of the Bible. "Seek ye me, and ye shall live" (Amos 5:4). The subjects of religion will never be able to know for sure that they are going to Heaven. There are so many hoops to jump through, so many prayers to say, so many signs of the cross to make, and so many other requirements that it is humanly impossible to know them all and do them. How could the Israelites know if they had taken enough trips and given the right amount of offerings? How can a religious person today ever know if they have done enough?

God makes Salvation so simple: "He that hath the Son hath life; *and* he that hath not the Son of God hath not life. These things have I written unto you that believe on the name of the Son of God; that ye may know that ye have eternal life, and that ye may believe on the name of the Son of God" (1 John 5:12-13). "For whosoever shall call upon the name of the Lord shall be saved" (Romans 10:13).

Simple. Plain. Clear. There is no ancient language to learn. There is no special prayer to offer. There is no 'holy water' needed. Believe on Christ.

Religion doesn't have a clue. The Biblical ignorance of the people under the 'teaching ministry' of 'Reverend' Amaziah was palpable. It was so lacking that Amos had to preach these words: "Woe unto you that desire the day of the LORD! to what end *is* it for you? the day of the LORD *is* darkness, and not light" (Amos 5:18).

Foolishly, the people convinced themselves the Day of the Lord was a thing to be enjoyed, so much so they "desire(d)" it. They were so ignorant of the Bible that they did not understand what they were talking about. How could they possibly desire (the same word is translated "covet" in the Ten Commandments) the greatest time of judgment in world history? One can picture Amos shaking his head and saying, "The day of the LORD *is* darkness, and not light. You don't know what you are talking about."

Imagine celebrating a time that will result in the death of half of the world's population. Imagine celebrating a "day of wrath, a day of trouble and distress, a day of wasteness and desolation, a day of darkness and gloominess, a day of clouds and thick darkness" (Zephaniah 1:15). Imagine celebrating a "day of trouble, and of treading down, and of perplexity by the Lord GOD of hosts in the valley of vision, breaking down the walls, and of crying to the mountains" (Isaiah 22:5).

Not long ago, before I stood up to preach in a revival meeting, some ladies sang these words:

Let the weak say, "I am strong"
Let the poor say, "I am rich"
Let the blind say, "I can see"
It's what the Lord has done in me.[29]

Do people ever stop and consider the lyrics of the music? Notice the words: "Let the weak say, 'I am strong.'" Joel 3:10 is the only verse in the Bible that uses this phrase. The statement, if one would actually take time to open the Bible, is spoken by the armies of the Antichrist as they rise to battle the coming Messiah. It is literally the battlecry of Satan's king as he wars against Christ.

Imagine taking the 'call to arms' of the Antichrist and turning it into a song! Imagine singing that song in a Baptist Church! Is there any wonder the book says, "My people are destroyed for lack of knowledge" (Hosea 4:6)?

If it weren't so sad it would almost be funny. Amos said it was "as if a man did flee from a lion, and a bear met him; or went into the house, and leaned his hand on the wall, and a serpent bit him" (Amos 5:19).

What a perfect illustration! Amos tells them to picture a man that is running for his life from a roaring lion. He gives the lion the slip only to be looking in the face of a raging bear. Once again, he is on his high horse barely escaping to his house. There he takes out his handkerchief, wipes the perspiration from his forehead, and tells his wife, "You wouldn't believe the day that I had!" Then he leans on the wall where a poisonous snake bites him.

Sunday morning rolls around and people head out to their 'worship centers' where they will 'celebrate' something. It may be Christmas, Easter, or the Super Bowl, but the important thing is that people 'celebrate.' Do they know the word 'celebrate' is not in the Bible? Stunned, they might ask, "What are we supposed to do in church?"

This might be a good place to start:

> *"Preach the word;*
> *be instant in season, out of season;*
> *reprove, rebuke, exhort*
> *with all longsuffering and doctrine"*
> *(2 Timothy 4:2).*

Religion is all about the show. The people in the Amos' day joined their head priest Amaziah in creating a religion of big business. There were popular "feast days" where the people assembled to eat and enjoy each other. One of the more sensuous experiences was the sweet smell of the incense that wafted up toward heaven. Of course, the people brought the requisite offerings. How can one be right with God without paying the price? They gathered to hear the praise teams sing and the orchestra play on their strings.

Food. Incense. Offerings. Music. Where is the Word of God?

One does not have to read very far to see what God thought about their religion:

"I hate, I despise your feast days, and I will not smell in your solemn assemblies. Though ye offer me burnt offerings and your meat offerings, I will not accept them: neither will I regard the

peace offerings of your fat beasts. Take thou away from me the noise of thy songs; for I will not hear the melody of thy viols. But let judgment run down as waters, and righteousness as a mighty stream. Have ye offered unto me sacrifices and offerings in the wilderness forty years, O house of Israel? But ye have borne the tabernacle of your Moloch and Chiun your images, the star of your god, which ye made to yourselves. Therefore will I cause you to go into captivity beyond Damascus, saith the LORD, whose name is The God of hosts" (Amos 5:21-27).

There are ten times in these verses that God uses the second person pronoun. He told them, "It is your feast days; your solemn assemblies; your meat offerings; your fat beasts: your songs; your viols." Their religion was the product of their own thinking and imagination. They invented a form of worship and then had the gall to insist that God accept it on their terms.

But God did not accept their 'worship.' In fact, He said, "I hate, I despise your feast days. I will not accept (your offerings). I will not hear the melody of thy viols." To God, their music was nothing but "noise."

God detested their religion. He promised His righteous judgment would run like a mighty river against them. For forty years, their forefathers had worshipped Him in the wilderness, yet they decided to reject the faith of their fathers. Instead, they looked at the world around them and found gods like the Molech, the national god of the Ammonites. Their desire was to mix their faith with their world and create a populist religion, but though this may have pleased their neighbors, they offended God. In no uncertain terms He told them their false religion would be the catalyst that would ultimately bring them into captivity. He punctuated His promise by using this name: "The God of hosts." The God of the heavenly armies would fight against them.

I recall sitting on an airplane en route to my home in Phoenix, Arizona. A woman sitting next to me had a testimony of salvation, and in the course of conversation, she told me she was a member of one of the largest churches in the valley. Then she said this: "Last Sunday, our pastor told us a strange thing. He told us not to bring our Bibles to church next Sunday. He said that unchurched people get offended when they see people carrying their Bibles. Instead, he told us to bring a copy of Rick Warren's latest book and we would study from that."

I can't help but wonder what God thought of that idea. Then again, I don't need to wonder. Amos told me.

Religion lulls people to complacency. It is the end result of man-created religion. Amos preached it like this: "Woe to them *that are* at ease in Zion, and trust in the mountain of Samaria, *which are* named chief of the nations, to whom the house of Israel came" (Amos 6:1). The people were living in a false state of security. Because they were a chief nation, they assumed everyone feared them, but little did they realize how perilous were the days in which they lived.

One writer illustrated their condition like this:

We see the distinction in a military setting. Imagine a group of soldiers on a hot march. They have finished the day's work, and as they march into camp the command goes out: "At ease!" Then: "Dismissed!" There is nothing wrong with that rest. It is well earned. But this is a far different thing from the ease that characterized the military forces of the United States at Pearl Harbor, Hawaii, on December 7, 1941. For many that ease proved fatal.[30]

It is interesting to note how Amos brings his own people back in the country of Judah into this scenario. While the Israelites to the north trusted in their military strength, Judah was trusting in the fact that they lived in Zion (or Jerusalem). They believed that God's temple and David's throne were in the great city, so God would preserve it at all costs. One nation was saying, "We are safe because of our military." The other nation believed, "We are safe because of our religion."

Their condition manifested itself in many ways. When they looked at the "mountain of Samaria," they assumed no army could ever attack them. Samaria was at the top of a steep hill. The ancient town was protected by thick walls that could hardly be approached even with a battering ram due to their elevation. The only approach was by a winding road that made its way up one side of the hill and entered the city through a set of multiple fortifications.[31] That mighty mountain protected them from harm, and it fueled a people who were "rich, and increased with goods, and (had) need of nothing" (Revelation 3:17).

They refused to learn the lesson of world history (Amos 6:2). The mighty city of Calneh fell to the Assyrian army. "Hamath the great" was a mighty empire that stood for more than six centuries but it was destroyed. The Philistine strongholds of Gath were broken down (2 Chronicles 26:6). Amos informed them they were no "better" than these kingdoms. It has been said that the 'only thing we learn from history is that we don't learn from history.' Amos would agree.

They talked themselves into putting "far away the evil day" (Amos 6:3). They deceived themselves into thinking that if they simply didn't think about it, it would never come, yet that very attitude caused "the seat of violence to come near."

Then they responded to God's warnings by living the party life. "That lie upon beds of ivory, and stretch themselves upon their couches, and eat the lambs out of the flock, and the calves out of the midst of the stall; That chant to the sound of the viol, *and* invent to themselves instruments of musick, like David; That drink wine in bowls, and anoint themselves with the chief ointments" (Amos 6:4-6).

The description in the verses described an ancient feast called a 'mazerah,' a celebration usually dedicated to a pagan god which often included acts of sexual perversion.[32] Their beds made of ivory boasted of their great riches. On those beds the citizens would lazily stretch themselves out demonstrating yet again their lackadaisical attitude. Their meals consisted of the finest lambs and fattened calves from the stalls, an affront to the average citizen who could afford such meat only three times a year at special feast days. There was so much leisure time that they invented music instruments and imagined themselves like David.

Then there was the booze. They were such drunks they didn't even waste the time in pouring it into glasses. They gulped it down straight from the storage bowls. They purchased extremely expensive ointments as only the best would do. Their extravagance and opulence blinded them from the needs around them, and they refused to be "grieved for the affliction of Joseph" (Amos 6:6). Every warning of the wrath of God was met with a hearty "it will never happen to us."

So the Bible says, "The Lord GOD hath sworn by himself, saith the LORD the God of hosts" (Amos 6:8). God is raising His hand and taking an oath by His own name. It is the most binding of all oaths. God is going to swear by His character, His power, His integrity, and His name: "I abhor...and hate...therefore will I deliver up the city with all that is therein...they shall die...he will smite the great house with breaches...I will raise up against you a nation, O house of Israel, saith the LORD the God of hosts; and they shall afflict you" (Amos 6:8-14).

No wonder the professional minister was so upset. No wonder he wanted Amos to "flee away." Amos did not 'agree to disagree.' He exposed their false worship. He condemned their worldly lifestyles. He did not portray a god they were comfortable with. He told the truth about God's wrath.

They didn't like it then. And they don't like it now.

Chapter Nine

Visions

THE SECOND WORD of the book of Amos calls this book the "words" of Amos. God allowed His man to hear the words He wanted delivered, and Amos responded by preaching them and writing them down. But Amos 7 brings a change to the method of God's inspiration. Amos is not only going to hear the message, he is going to see it.

The final three chapters contain five visions with vivid messages for the people to hear and see. "Thus hath the Lord GOD shewed unto me" (Amos 7:1). Amos is not having a dream nor is he hallucinating. The visions are very real.

Vision #1 - The Vision of the Grasshoppers
"Behold, he formed grasshoppers
in the beginning of the shooting up of the latter growth;
and, lo, it was the latter growth
after the king's mowings" (Amos 7:1).

Amos watched as God 'forms' grasshoppers. It is the very word used in Genesis 2:7 when "the LORD God *formed* man *of* the dust of the ground." The emphasis is on the timing of the grasshoppers, as they arrive in the month of April just in time for the "latter growth." The tax levied by the king on this agricultural society was the first harvest. The people then replanted the fields and lived off the second harvest. They had an effective tax rate of 50%.

When the rains are just right and desert circumstances come together, grasshoppers can swarm and become a mortal enemy to humans. These swarming grasshoppers are known as locusts.

"The insects, which normally live alone, begin bumping into one another. When grasshoppers touch one another's hind legs, the contact sets off hormonal changes: The adults' neutral brown coloring is replaced with a fearsome bright yellow, and they become "gregarious" group insects, coordinating their growth, behavior and egg laying. When the swarm devours all of the surrounding vegetation, it takes to the air, traveling up to 100 miles a day in search of its next meal."[33]

According to a senior locust forecasting officer at the United Nations Food and Agriculture Organization in Rome, (apparently such a job exists), a locust swarm the size of Manhattan would eat the same amount of food that 42 million humans would consume.[34]

It was a disaster of Biblical proportion. These swarming grasshoppers "made an end of eating the grass of the land" (Amos 7:2). The destruction was complete. God just wiped their harvest out and there would be an enormous famine in the land. Their economy would fly off with the locusts. There was about to be a lot of suffering.

So the man of God, Amos, intervened. "Then I said, O Lord GOD, forgive, I beseech thee: by whom shall Jacob arise? for he *is* small." When disaster is about to strike, there is no time for long, wordy prayers. Amos simply pleads with God. He asks Him to forgive the people and reminds Him that Israel is small. They were a little country of little population who possessed little power. There were a lot of little people, children included, that would suffer agonizing hardships if these grasshoppers destroyed their food.

The LORD heard him. "The LORD repented for this: It shall not be, saith the LORD" (Amos 7:3).

It wasn't the first time God repented. "And God sent an angel unto Jerusalem to destroy it: and as he was destroying, the LORD beheld, and he repented him of the evil, and said to the angel that destroyed, It is enough, stay now thine hand" (1 Chronicles 21:15). " And he remembered for them his covenant, and repented according to the multitude of his mercies" (Psalm 106:45). "And God saw their works, that they turned from their evil way; and God repented of the evil, that he had said that he would do unto them; and he did *it* not" (Jonah 3:10).

Astounding! God repents! It is verses like this one that makes me glad I am not a Calvinist. Our feeble human minds cannot comprehend the 'hows and whys' of God repenting of His judgment, yet we can understand the big picture. God repented because God loves mercy and forgiveness. God repented because He loves people. They had rebelled against Him and rejected His grace but still He loved them.

Vision #2 - The Vision of the Fire
"Thus hath the Lord GOD shewed unto me:
and, behold, the Lord GOD called to contend by fire,
and it devoured the great deep,
and did eat up a part" (Amos 7:4).

Vision number two was more fearful than the first vision. Our attention is immediately drawn to the word "contend." God is going to fight with fire. He promised it would be so intense it would lick up their water supply, a fire so severe it would devour part of the Mediterranean Sea - their idea of the 'great deep.'

Once again, the man of God comes to the rescue. Perhaps Amos figured if it worked the first time it might work the second time, so he implores God. The first time he asked God to "forgive" but this time he uses a different word. "O Lord GOD, cease, I beseech thee: by whom shall Jacob arise? for he *is* small" (Amos 7:5). With the fire of God ready to fall upon the land there is only time for Amos to beg God to "cease."

And once again "the LORD repented for this" (Amos 7:6). For the second time the wrath of God is replaced by the mercy of God. God is not simply merciful; He abounds with mercy!

"For thy mercy *is* great unto the heavens" (Psalm 57:10). "For thou, Lord, *art* good, and ready to forgive; and plenteous in mercy unto all them that call upon thee" (Psalm 86:5). "He retaineth not his anger for ever, because he delighteth *in* mercy" (Micah 7:18).

The glorious mercy of God is extended again and again, yet there is a limit to His mercy. The invitation only lasts so long. He repented of the famine. He repented of the fire. What could be next?

Vision #3 - The Vision of the Plumbline

Thus he shewed me: and, behold,
the Lord stood upon a wall made by a plumbline,
with a plumbline in his hand.
And the LORD said unto me, Amos, what seest thou?
And I said, A plumbline. Then said the Lord,
Behold, I will set a plumbline in the midst of my people Israel:
I will not again pass by them any more" (Amos 7:7-8).

Imagine you were part of the crowd listening to the visions of the man of God. You are a man struggling to put food on the table for your family and you hear of a swarm of locusts about ready to destroy your crops. God repents and you feel you have dodged a bullet. Then Amos preaches that God is ready to burn your country down. As the panic attack nears you discover that God has repented a second time and you are flooded with relief.

Now Amos says he has a third vision from God. You are bracing for what most certainly is bad news. What could possibly be next? A drought? An earthquake? An asteroid?

And Amos says that God is holding a plumbline in His hand. Even if you are not sure what a plumbline is, you would convince yourself that it couldn't be too bad.

Standing on a wall with a plumbline. A plumbline was an ancient version of a carpenter's level. If there were concerns about an old sagging wall or if a new wall was being built, the plumbline would ensure it was straight. It was a string attached to a metal weight. The worker would hold the top of the string and drop the weight. When it stopped moving, there was a perpendicular line that could be laid next to the wall. In a sense, a good wall would line up to the plumbline; a bad wall would not.

God said, "I will set a plumbline in the midst of my people Israel." I imagine the crowd thought, "That is fine so long as You don't ruin the economy or burn us down." But this was far more serious to God than it was to the people. He added the words, "I will not again pass by them any more." They didn't know it at the time, but they were getting their last chance. God told them that when He was done with the plumbline, He was done passing by them. Their last chance to repent would be gone. His abounding, protracted mercy would finally come to an end.

So what was the 'plumbline?' To what standard does God expect people to 'line up'? What does He "set" in the midst of the people so they will know what to do and how to live?

"He that rejecteth me, and receiveth not my words, hath one that judgeth him: the word that I have spoken, the same shall judge him in the last day" (John 12:48).

God gave them His word from the mouth of Amos and similar prophets, and they summarily dismissed the Word of God. Their last chance was about to be frittered away and the final opportunity for the mercy of God would be squandered. At such time, God promised that "the high places of Isaac shall be desolate, and the sanctuaries of Israel shall be laid waste; and I will rise against the house of Jeroboam with the sword" (Amos 7:9). Their stately buildings, their houses of sacred religion, and the very palace of the king would be ruined. The destruction would be total.

Then the 'fat hit the fire.' Amos finally crossed the line and Reverend Amaziah, the priest of Bethel, couldn't take it anymore. The seminary was about to go into meltdown mode. The appropriate word would be 'apoplectic.'

Chapter Ten

The Pro vs. The Prophet

DOCTOR AMAZIAH finally had his ammunition. He was patiently waiting for Amos to say the wrong thing and now he had the goods. The man of God spoke God's promise: "I will rise against the house of Jeroboam with the sword." Amaziah couldn't get the report to the king fast enough.

"Then Amaziah the priest of Bethel sent to Jeroboam king of Israel, saying, Amos hath conspired against thee in the midst of the house of Israel: the land is not able to bear all his words. For thus Amos saith, Jeroboam shall die by the sword, and Israel shall surely be led away captive out of their own land" (Amos 7:10-11).

The 'reverend' accused the prophet of God of conspiracy, a very serious charge with political overtones. It begs the question, exactly who did Amos conspire with? It would appear the only answer to that question would be

Jehovah, and in truth, God and the prophet were jointly standing against the king.

By accusing Amos, he was implying an act of treason against the king. Amaziah claimed that the preaching of the prophet was so divisive the land could no longer stand it - like a flood that could not be contained.

But Amaziah was a liar. He informed the king that Amos had said "Jeroboam shall die by the sword." That is not what he said. He said, "I will rise against *the house* of Jeroboam with the sword." There is no record in the book of Amos where he ever prophesied that Jereboam would die a horrific death, and history indicates that he died peacefully. He also conveniently forgot the intercession on the part of Amos when the judgment was ready to fall upon the land. Instead, he had to paint Amos with a brush that put him in the worst light possible. If he had to lie, misquote, or twist words, what did it matter?

The real problem is that Amaziah did not recognize the authority behind Amos. He referred to the messages as "his words." But they were not 'his words,' they were God's words, and by standing in opposition to the prophet of God, the high priest of Bethel was actually opposing God.

After 'informing' the king, Amaziah turns his venom on the preacher. "O thou seer, go, flee thee away into the land of Judah, and there eat bread, and prophesy there: But prophesy not again any more at Bethel: for it *is* the king's chapel, and it *is* the king's court" (Amos 7:12-13).

We can almost hear the derision as he calls Amos a "seer," yet that is the correct description. Amos was seeing visions from God and then reporting them. Amaziah was using the phrase to ridicule but once again, he was more accurate than he realized.

Then he tells Amos to run back home and "there eat bread." What an enlightening comment! Amaziah looked at the ministry as a means of putting food on the table. It was nothing more than a job. He assumed that Amos was just like him, so he told him to go earn his bread somewhere else. It never dawns upon ministers like Amaziah that some people do not preach for money; they preach because God called them. As he had never heard the voice of God nor seen a vision from God, he could not fathom a man of God who had experienced such revelation. So he exercised his right as the "priest of Bethel" to tell Amos where to preach, what to preach, and how to preach.

These attacks are fascinating. When a Bible preacher is criticized, the caricature is always of a man who is unloving, critical, and attacking. But who is on the offensive here? Who is 'pharisaical' here? Who is judgmental here? It is true that Amos' preaching is penetrating and bold, but it is also accurate. He is not presuming. He is not making things up. Amaziah is the man with the critical spirit!

Modern churches that try to be "seeker friendly" have set themselves up to look like innocent victims. They are the only ones who love people. They are the only folks that are trying to depart from the rigid, hateful divisiveness of the past. But is that accurate?

Many of the churches who are seeking the world's approval were built on the backs of faithful servants of Christ. They gave for years, often sacrificially, to support the ministry. Then one Sunday, a pastor stands up and dictates that the church is going to sing music the world likes, develop a ministry the world likes, and use bibles that the world likes. They are going to eliminate preaching, change the name of the church, toss the hymnals in the attic, sell the organ, offer earplugs to the old people that find the thumping guitars too loud, build 'small group fellowships' instead of a local church assembly, call the pastor by his first name, and wear casual clothes.

The people that gave and labored and supplied the need are now told they have two choices. They can accept the compromise or they can leave, and as they are being ushered out the door, they are condemned as unloving pharisees.

Is that loving? Is that what 'Jesus would do'?

It is not a secret plan. The 'gurus' of the mega-church movement have been quite upfront and open about their advice in instructing their ministers in the methods of taking over a church. They are told to deceitfully change the church over the course of time. There may be subtle changes, there may be major changes, but it is a man jamming a new philosophy down the throats of the people. And if they don't like it? This is how one of the gurus, Dan Southerland, tells them how to handle that problem:

Pastors are taught that objectors are "Sanballats" whom Southerland calls "leaders from hell". He goes on to write, "You cannot call this guy a leader from hell to his face, but you can call him a Sanballat"...Southerland teaches that the traditional members who are pillars of the church can just hold you back from the changes, and fight your methods. He and (Rick) Warren are proud of the numbers they've chased off. "When you set the vision and stay the course, you determine who leaves."[35]

Just kick them out. That will take care of the old people problem. "We have all the money from you that we need, so why don't you just leave. We don't care about the Sunday School classes you have taught. We don't care about the missionaries you have supported. We don't care about the souls you have led to Christ and discipled. Get on board or get out."

So where is the love?

It was time for Amos to answer. He was succinct and straightforward with a direct message from God to Amaziah: "Now therefore hear thou the word of the LORD: Thou sayest, Prophesy not against Israel, and drop not *thy word* against the house of Isaac. Therefore thus saith the LORD; Thy wife shall be an harlot in the city, and thy sons and thy daughters shall fall by the sword, and thy land shall be divided by line; and thou shalt die in a polluted land: and Israel shall surely go into captivity forth of his land" (Amos 7:16-17).

It is the first time that Amos preached directly to an individual. He had, of course, condemned the sins of the land, the sins of the castle, and the sins of the religious leadership, but this message was for Amaziah alone. In so doing, Amos joined the small company of Bible prophets who preached without fear of consequence. He allied himself with Nathan, Elijah, Micaiah, Elisha and Paul as choice men of God who were not afraid to name the wicked.

Amaziah did not want a preacher who was "against" anything. He was offended that Amos preached "against" Israel and "against" the house of Isaac. Not only was he condemning the sins of the northern kingdom of Israel, but his home nation of Judah was also included. For a minister like Amaziah who was living for the paycheck, it was intolerable to allow a minister to be so reckless. But the man who did not want a preacher to preach "against" his land was about to hear a message from God that was "against" him.

He prophesied that the family of Amaziah would fall apart. When the enemy attacked, his own wife would prostitute herself in order to live. His children would die by the Assyrian sword, and his proud, priestly line would be exterminated. The land of Israel would be divvied up and the lines on the map would indicate new kingdoms. As for Amaziah, he would be carried away captive to a pagan land. For all of the priestly rituals and ceremonies he followed to stay clean, his ignominious death in a foreign land meant he would be buried in polluted ground.

The day finally came. "Then the king of Assyria came up throughout all the land, and went up to Samaria, and besieged it three years. In the ninth year of Hoshea the king of Assyria took Samaria, and carried Israel away into Assyria, and placed them in Halah and in Habor *by* the river of Gozan, and in the cities of the Medes" (2 Kings 17:5-6).

I wonder what Amaziah thought then?

Chapter Eleven

"He Was There All The Time..."

THERE WERE TWO FINAL VISIONS for the man of God. As the visions are delivered, it is interesting to note the various responses of Amos. At first, he carried on a conversation with God, but as the visions become more somber and the havoc becomes inevitable, Amos speaks very little. He has already done his part by pleading with God to show mercy, yet the Amaziahs of the land seemed to seal the doom. From here on, God would do the talking.

Vision #4 - The Vision of the Fruit Basket
"Thus hath the Lord GOD shewed unto me:
and behold a basket of summer fruit.
And he said, Amos, what seest thou?
And I said, A basket of summer fruit." (Amos 8:1-2)

There is no grasshopper destroying the crops. There is no fire burning down the land. The nation has failed its 'plumbline' test, so God sends them a fruit basket. It would seem an innocuous thing until one read the attached card:

"The end is come upon my people of Israel; I will not again pass by them any more."

It was over. The last chance was gone. The last invitation verse had been sung. The service was dismissed. God was not going to pass that way again.

The basket of "summer fruit" contained the final crop of the year in the Fall harvest. Soon the cold winds would blow, the trees would be stripped bare, and the people would settle in for winter. It would be too late to gather another harvest. It would be too late to repent. Centuries later, the prophet Jeremiah would put it like this: "The harvest is past, the summer is ended, and we are not saved" (Jeremiah 8:20).

The beautiful, stately music of the temple would turn to "howlings" - loud wails that express deep mourning or distress.[36] There was coming a day when there would be "many dead bodies in every place," and all of the bustle and activity would turn to a deathly "silence" (Amos 8:3). They had "swallow(ed) up the needy" and made "the poor of the land to fail" (Amos 8:4) one time too many. By their greed, they had mocked the great command of keeping the Sabbath holy. Not only did they turn the Lord's day into a day of profit, but it also became a time of "deceit" (Amos 8:5) as they used false measures in the market and weighed produce on crooked balances. They sold the "refuse" of wheat, the trash they picked up off the floor.

They were trafficking humans for pennies on the dollars, and the ones who once sold the poor for a pair of shoes were now buying them "for a pair of shoes" (Amos 8:6).

Once again the LORD lifted up His hand to make an oath. Normally, God would swear by His name or by one of His attributes, but this time He swore "by the excellency of Jacob" (Amos 8:7). The greatest possession Israel had was their land; it was a gift from God.[37] He is saying, "As surely as I gave you this mighty land as part of My agreement with you, you have violated your promise. I will not forget." He proceeded to tell them the land would "tremble" and the people would "mourn."

"I will never forget... I will cause the sun to go down...I will darken the earth in the clear day...I will turn your feasts into mourning...I will bring up sackcloth upon all loins...I will make it as the mourning of an only *son*, and the end thereof as a bitter day" (Amos 8:7-10). When God was finished judging them, every head would be shaved bald symbolizing the mourning, grieving nation that had lost an "only son." Losing an "only son" meant the deepest occasion of sorrow imaginable.[38] It was truly a "bitter day."

We have been taught that God "was there all the time... waiting patiently in line."[39] Soothing ministers want to cushion any mention in the Bible of judgment. Christian entertainers convince people they can have God on their own terms. But it is not so. God is not 'there all the time.' There comes a moment when God says you have just tipped over the basket of summer fruit, and there are no more harvests.

But what follows is perhaps the most stunning truth in the book of Amos. In no uncertain terms, Amos preached that God had delivered the final opportunity. God swore by the land that they were done. Yet, even though Amos delivered that message somewhere between 760-755 BC, Israel was not conquered until 722 BC. More than thirty years passed between the vision of Amos and the three year siege that fulfilled the prophecies of God's prophet. King Jereboam died after a successful reign of some forty years, and six more kings followed him. Most of those years were times of affluence, and had they a "Prosperity Gospel" model then, its messengers would have told its listeners to "name it and claim it." Amos preached that the end was near, but the party went on for more than three decades.

It was during those years that God sent the most calamitous, destructive judgment on the land of Israel. It would be impossible to describe the depths of His wrath or comprehend the havoc it created. It was a far, far more catastrophic disaster than any grasshopper or fire could produce. Its ramifications would last for eternity.

There was a famine in the land.

Oh, it wasn't "a famine of bread, nor a thirst for water" (Amos 8:11). There was plenty of water in the well and the shelves at the market were well stocked. The people went to bed with full stomachs.

But there was a famine "of hearing the words of the LORD," a famine of the Bible. The people chose to listen to Amaziah and reject Amos, and in so doing, they were shunning the one man fearless enough to tell them the truth. They wanted a popular preacher, not a Bible preacher. They wanted a proper message, not a convicting message. They wanted to prosper, not repent.

It is the problem with ministers like Amaziah. They may pack auditoriums with their smooth words. They may be well liked to the point where they are invited to pray at the king's inaugural and then join him for a round of golf. They may be 'good ole' boys', but they produce a cataclysmic situation in the land all the more dangerous because no one sees it coming nor comprehends its reach. Their product is a famine of the Bible in the land.

We hear dire statistics detailing declining church attendance. While it is true that a smaller percentage of American people are going to church on a weekly basis, there are still a lot of people going to houses of religion. According to a Gallup survey, 128 million Americans go to a church service on an average week (not Christmas or Easter).[40] We decry the millions of people who have plenty of time for golf and hunting and fishing but no time for God, yet the 128 million people that went to church last Sunday far surpasses the 86 million who will golf or fish or hunt this year.[41] We lament the idea that sports have replaced God in our land, yet last Sunday, on that one day alone, more people went to church than will go to NFL, NBA, and Major League Baseball stadiums for the entire year. In the week leading up to the 2015 Super Bowl, more people read their Bible than watched the championship game on TV.[42] Last week, for every one person that went to a movie, more than five people went to church. For every one McDonalds we have in America there are 24 churches.

For every one Walmart there are 80 churches.[43] Those who predict that the days of religion in America are over are seriously misinformed.

We have religion, but we also have a famine of the Bible. A person may go to a religious center, listen to a minister for a few minutes, yet know nothing about God's word because most teachers in America blatantly disregard the command to "Preach the word" (2 Timothy 4:2). Often, the false minister will use the Bible as a prop. People instinctively know they are supposed to see the Bible in church, so a minister like Joel Osteen holds up a Bible and says, "This is my Bible. I am what it says I am. I can do what it says I can do. Today, I will be taught the Word of God."[44] He then goes on to give a populist speech that would make any psychologist proud.

Some churches have replaced a "pulpit of wood" (Nehemiah 8:4)[45] with a lectern of glass, and in the process, they have "heap(ed) to themselves teachers, having itching ears" (2 Timothy 4:3). They love the teachers who tell them what they want to hear; not what they need to hear. Sunday mornings are times for plays, programs, concerts, and entertainment, and though people are physically sitting in a religious building, they are not getting the Bible. The end result is a nation of religious people who are ignorant of the Book.

Americans have great respect for the Bible. Despite the constant attacks, 56% of the American people believe the Bible is the Word of God and without error. 88% of American homes own at least one Bible. In homes that have Bibles, there are an average of 4.7 of them. If you run all the numbers there are well over a half *billion* Bibles sitting on coffee tables and in bookshelves.

There are more Bibles and more religious halls than ever, but there is a great problem. Of those who own Bibles, only 37% read them at least once last week. Of those that read the Bible only 57% gave any thought as to how it applies in their life. For all the people who own a Bible and say they believe the Bible, 75% have never read it through.

In other words, some 135,783,659 adults in America would point to the Bible and say, "That book is the perfect Word of God." But of those people, 101,837,744 of them haven't cared enough to read it through. What a sad parallel between the religious throngs in our day and the followers of Amaziah in Israel's day. "My people are destroyed for lack of knowledge" (Hosea 4:6).

But there is something else even more stunning in Amos' prophecy:

"I will send a famine."

God sent the famine.

You read that correctly. *God sent the famine.* There was a famine of the hearing of God's word and that famine came from God.

Most people think the judgment of God comes in the form of hurricanes and earthquakes and tornados and floods and blizzards and avalanches and tsunamis. We look to the book of Revelation and read about swarming creatures "like unto horses prepared unto battle; and on their heads *were* as it were crowns like gold, and their faces *were* as the faces of men. And they had hair as the hair of women, and their teeth were as *the teeth* of lions. And they had breastplates, as it were breastplates of iron; and the sound of their wings *was* as the sound of chariots of many horses running to battle. And they had tails like unto scorpions, and there were stings in their tails: and their power *was* to hurt men five months" (Revelation 9:7-10). When a natural catastrophe occurs, even the unsaved man will refer to it as a judgment of "Biblical proportions."

But who ever thought that God would judge people by causing them to be ignorant of the Word of God? In effect God was telling them, "You have rejected my man. You have rejected my word. You have rejected my visions. You have rejected me. I will 'give you up' to your own ways. I will give you the religion you crave, but it will be powerless in the day of trouble. Worse, it will be impotent in the Day of Judgment."[46] They thirsted for a religion without the Bible, so God gave it to them. One day, their personal brand of religion would lead them straight to Hell.

It would seem that the episode of chapter seven was far more significant than the people first thought. Maybe some laughed at the verbal dressing down Amaziah gave Amos. Perhaps others dismissed him with a 'good riddance.' But the day was coming when they would wish they had an Amos to go to: "And they shall wander from sea to sea, and from the north even to the east, they shall run to and fro to seek the word of the LORD, and shall not find *it*" (Amos 8:12). When the wheels were falling off and the

Assyrian army was destroying the land, Israel finally decided, as a last ditch effort, to see if anybody could get a message from God. Amaziah had no answer. Amos was nowhere to be found. Heaven was silent.

And they discovered all too late that God was not "there all the time."

Chapter Twelve

No Where To Hide

THERE WAS ONE LAST VISION which the Lord delivered while "standing upon the altar" (Amos 9:1). While it behooves us constantly to heed Him, we as humans should take special note when God rises and stands.

Normally, God would visit an altar to indicate approval and acceptance of a human offering. It was the place where sacrifices would be offered for sin and humans could be reconciled to God; where sweet savors would waft to His holy nostrils. But there was no mercy to be found in Amos 9. He was rising to give the ultimate verdict against the nation of Israel and their religion.

Vision #5 - The Vision of the Altar
"I saw the Lord standing upon the altar:
and he said, Smite the lintel of the door, that the posts may shake:
and cut them in the head, all of them;
and I will slay the last of them with the sword:

he that fleeth of them shall not flee away,
and he that escapeth of them shall not be delivered." (Amos 9:1)

Though we don't know to whom God was speaking, the message is clear enough. The command was to strike the lintel, the support at the top of the pillars. In so doing, the entire house of religion would crumble and the temple at Bethel would be destroyed.[47] The worshipers inside would be killed, and those trying to escape from God would find no where to hide. They were to be killed to the very "last of them."

"Though they dig into hell, thence shall mine hand take them; though they climb up to heaven, thence will I bring them down: And though they hide themselves in the top of Carmel, I will search and take them out thence; and though they be hid from my sight in the bottom of the sea, thence will I command the serpent, and he shall bite them: And though they go into captivity before their enemies, thence will I command the sword, and it shall slay them: and I will set mine eyes upon them for evil, and not for good" (Amos 9:2-4).

No where to run. God would see to that. When He finally judged the false religion of Israel there was no mistaking His personal accountability. "Mine hand take them...thence will I bring them down...I will search and take them out thence... thence will I command the serpent...thence will I command the sword...I will set mine eyes upon them for evil, and not for good." This would not be an accident of nature.

Humans convince themselves they can hide from God, but there is nowhere to go. In Hell, in Heaven, at the top of the mightiest mountains, at the bottom of the sea, or in a distant prison camp, Israel could not hide from Him. "Whither shall I go from thy spirit? or whither shall I flee from thy presence? If I ascend up into heaven, thou *art* there: if I make my bed in hell, behold, thou *art there. If* I take the wings of the morning, *and* dwell in the uttermost parts of the sea; Even there shall thy hand lead me, and thy right hand shall hold me. If I say, Surely the darkness shall cover me; even the night shall be light about me. Yea, the darkness hideth not from thee; but the night shineth as the day: the darkness and the light *are* both alike *to thee"* (Psalm 139:7-12).

Righteous people are comforted by the fact that God is watching over them. In these days of trouble and danger, it is a great blessing to claim this promise: "The eyes of the LORD *are* upon the righteous, and his ears *are open* unto their cry" (Psalm 34:15). The child of God rejoices to know that God sets His eyes on us for "good," but to the evil man His glare is for "evil." God sees and God knows.

The *Carnival of Basel* is the largest festival in Switzerland. Every year, during February or March, the revelers don masks and go to parties.[48] Hidden behind those masks, they often behave shamefully and sinfully, much as the Mardi Gras crowd does in New Orleans. A mask seems to convince a wicked man he can get away with sin.

One year, the Salvation Army, concerned about the abandonment of moral standards, put up signs all over the city which read:

"God sees behind the mask."[49]

God saw where they were hiding. God saw what they were doing. God always sees.

For the second time in the book of Amos, the man of God breaks out into a song of judgment. It is interesting to hear the lyrics of Amos and contrast them to music that fills churches today. While we seem interested in music that emphasizes our human experiences, Amos seemed far more concerned with exalting the character of God. We find a way to separate the 'song service' from the 'preaching,' yet with Amos, the singing joined the preaching to teach the people who God truly is.

"And the Lord GOD of hosts is he that toucheth the land, and it shall melt, and all that dwell therein shall mourn: and it shall rise up wholly like a flood; and shall be drowned, as by the flood of Egypt. It is he that buildeth his stories in the heaven, and hath founded his troop in the earth; he that calleth for the waters of the sea, and poureth them out upon the face of the earth: The LORD is his name." (Amos 9:5-6)

When the God of the armies 'touches' the land it simply melts before His power, a mighty picture of the greatest armies dissolving in His presence. He can call the seas and the mighty floods of waters to fight for Him. He rules the skies and the heavens and they bow to his bidding. He made Creation; He controls Creation; they are His "troop." It is nothing for Him to order His elements to turn the tide of any human battle as Pharaoh, the Philistines, and King Sennacherib and would readily admit.[50]

Through the course of the Old Testament, Israel to the north and their brothers to the south in Judah had convinced themselves that God was always on the side of Israel. Many a prophet sounded the alarm that God's protection was not an automatic thing, a warning that sounded like this: "*To wit*, the prophets of Israel which prophesy concerning Jerusalem, and which see visions of peace for her, and *there is* no peace, saith the Lord GOD" (Ezekiel 13:16).

Amos joined his brothers: "*Are* ye not as children of the Ethiopians unto me, O children of Israel? saith the LORD. Have not I brought up Israel out of the land of Egypt? and the Philistines from Caphtor, and the Syrians from Kir? Behold, the eyes of the Lord GOD *are* upon the sinful kingdom, and I will destroy it from off the face of the earth; saving that I will not utterly destroy the house of Jacob, saith the LORD. For, lo, I will command, and I will sift the house of Israel among all nations, like as *corn* is sifted in a sieve, yet shall not the least grain fall upon the earth. All the sinners of my people shall die by the sword, which say, The evil shall not overtake nor prevent us" (Amos 9:7-10).

He promised to deal with Israel as He had judged their neighbors. Convinced they were 'special' because God had rescued them in the past, Amos reminds them that God also rescued the Philistines and the Syrians from their foes.

Such a comparison to their hated enemies must have drawn an indignant reaction, but Amos would not relent. Their 'special' status would not keep them from the sifter of God's wrath.

It is a grave error to assume "evil shall not overtake nor prevent us," and when Amos warned the people of the impending wrath of God, the blinded citizenry did not repent. Worse, the false ministers like Amaziah indignantly did their best to muzzle the man of God. If it wasn't Amos, then it would be Micah or Jeremiah or Micaiah or Ezekiel who would get the same response.

Not long ago, my wife and I were driving on a busy Phoenix highway heading home after a preaching engagement. As a drunk driver passed us at a high rate of speed, she suddenly lost control of the car. Only the protecting Hand of God saved us that night. She barely missed us, finally crashing into the highway barrier with an explosion of glass and sparks. When the vehicle came to rest, its back end was dangerously impeding the first lane of the highway.

As cars were swerving to avoid hitting the vehicle and the debris which littered the highway, I made my way down the road, waving my arms, and imploring people to move into the center lane. While many drivers slowed and changed lanes, there was an alarming number that didn't seem to care. Incredulously, some laughed, some yelled, and one even responded to my warning with an obscene gesture, all the while speeding dangerously close to the accident up ahead. It is hard to imagine the foolishness of a man that won't listen to someone trying to save his life.

Men like Amos are parodied as hateful and divisive. They have no love for people. They are too judgmental. They are too critical. But when the dust settles, it is the man who told the truth who loves the people. The minister who won't warn the crowd may seem compassionate and amiable, but he doesn't care enough to flag down the traffic. Let them drive on to a greater disaster.

It is an Amos who loves people enough to warn them. It is an Amos who gives people an opportunity to experience the great mercy of God. It is an Amos that gives people their last chance.

Chapter Thirteen

Jesus And I

ON MARCH 31, 1980, nearly 13,000 boxing fans jammed into the Stokely Center on the campus of the University of Tennessee. Most of them had come to cheer on their favorite, "Big" John Tate, as he readied to make his first defense of the recently won heavyweight championship. His opponent, Michael Weaver, was so lightly regarded that one magazine writer referred to him as "Michael Who." Experts gave him no chance against the mighty champ.

From the opening bell, John Tate was in control. The massive crowd was screaming "Big John Tate" as he landed punch after punch, building an insurmountable lead. Michael Weaver was so far behind, that between the fourteenth and fifteenth round, he sat on his stool quoting the 23rd Psalm because he knew it would take a miracle to win the fight.

With less than a minute to go, Michael Weaver suddenly caught John Tate with a left hook. In boxing lore, it was a punch for the ages. It caught the champion square on the jaw, and with that one punch, "Big" John Tate went down. The stunned crowd watched the referee give the 'ten count,' and the fight was over. The impossible had happened, and Michael Weaver became the champ.[51]

The "Battle at Bethel" had an underdog as well. Standing against Amos was the ministerial association, the king and his court, the seminarians at Bethel, and volumes of spectators. He must have been a lonely man.

Amos did have one advantage that Amaziah and his cohorts did not have. The boxing community would call it the 'cornerman,' the trainer who applies the ice to reduce swelling, dresses cuts and bruises, and reminds the fighter of strategy. In Amos' corner was the LORD Jehovah, and as the book of Amos closes, we are reminded of the reasons Amos would win the fight. On his side were the promises of God.

"In that day will I raise up the tabernacle of David that is fallen, and close up the breaches thereof; and I will raise up his ruins, and I will build it as in the days of old...I will bring again the captivity of my people of Israel, and they shall build the waste cities, and inhabit them; and they shall plant vineyards, and drink the wine thereof; they shall also make gardens, and eat the fruit of them...I will plant them upon their land, and they shall no more be pulled up out of their land which I have given them, saith the LORD thy God" (Amos 9:11,14,15).

Winners like Amos focus on "that day." They know that Satan and his cohorts may seem to be winning today, but they recognize that the last round has not yet been fought. They may be battered, bloodied, and beaten, but they know the 'great left hook' is coming. They know when the final bell rings, the referee will be counting Satan out once and for all. They know who gets the championship belt.

They know the King is coming. Humans are impressed by royal palaces, but the day is coming where the focus will be on the king and not the kingdom. It is the reason the Bible says He will raise up the "tabernacle," a temporary shelter constructed of poles and palm branches built by a farmer to protect his crops.[52] History has proven repeatedly that kingdoms may appear mighty and invincible, but the greatest of them have "breaches." They are far more tenuous and delicate than they appear.

The King of Glory will raise up the nation of Israel and fulfill His many promises, bringing it out of the "ruins." History tells of nations giving Israel their best shot. The list is long and lengthy of those who joined Satan in assuring the Jews would never rise. Time and again, dictators and conquerors raised their flags of victory thinking Israel would be nothing but a distant memory, yet God found a way to raise the nation out of the dusty sands of the Middle East. The day is coming when it will return to the glory days of King David, as "days of old."

"The plowman shall overtake the reaper" (Amos 9:13). The harvest will be so abundant that when the crops are finally brought in it will be time to plant again. The vines of grapes will be so productive their fruit will seem like sweet waters flowing down a mountainside.

Then Amos delivered the promise of the ages to the people of Israel and to the Gentiles who will join them. "And I will plant them upon their land, and they shall no more be pulled up out of their land which I have given them, saith the LORD thy God" (Amos 9:15). The land of the promise given to Abraham centuries earlier will finally be theirs. They will have experienced their final captivity and their final dispersal. Israel will finally be home.

"What shall we then say to these things? If God *be* for us, who *can be* against us" (Romans 8:31)?

In 1886, a Scottish teenage, Daniel Crawford, responded to the Gospel and was saved. His life was immediately transformed and Christ became all to him. He loved and studied his Bible, boldly witnessed for Jesus, and willingly gave his life to serve Him.

The 1880's were a decade of missions. A few years earlier, David Livingston had died in the distant land of Africa, and now the field was opening to the Gospel. The leading of God could not be more evident for Daniel, and at the age of nineteen, he was off to serve His Lord in the great continent. Like Livingston, he would bury himself in the jungles of Africa and give his life to see souls saved. Twenty two years would pass before he took his one and only furlough.

For some 38 years, Crawford tirelessly served his Savior, translating the Bible into African tongues and leading many to the Christ. The multitudes loved him and gave him the nickname "Konga Vantu," which means "a gatherer of people." Thousands had been 'gathered' at the Cross by his faithful testimony. An infection led to his death at the age of 57, and with his life slipping away, his final message to the people he loved said, "Goodbye dear friends. We will meet at the 'appearing' in excellent glory."[53]

Everywhere he would go, Daniel Crawford carried his beloved New Testament. When he finally went home to Glory, someone took that book and opened to the flyleaf. There he had written these words:

"I cannot do it alone! The waves dash fast and high; the fog comes chill around, and the light goes out in the sky. But I know that we two shall win in the end—Jesus and I. Coward and wayward and weak, I change with the changing sky; today so strong and brave, tomorrow too weak to fly. But He never gives up, so we two shall win—Jesus and I!"

So Amos, tell us how to fight the battle. Tell us how to keep from discouragement. Tell us what to do when we are overwhelmed. Tell us how to respond when the waves of enemy attacks are encompassing us. Tell us what to do when the foe seems unbeatable.

And the old shepherd of Tekoa puts his shaky finger on Amos 9:14-15. He points to two simple phrases. God called Israel "my people." Then He said, "I am 'thy God.'"

Jesus and I. He is all we need.

Endnotes

[1] http://en.wikipedia.org/wiki/Mike_Tyson

[2] Finley, T. J. (2003). *Joel, Amos, Obadiah* (p. 99). Biblical Studies Press.

[3] Since the office of a prophet was not acquired by heredity, as was the priesthood, it is clear that the expression "son of a prophet" implies membership in a prophetic guild or organization (cf. 2 Kings 2:3, 5, 15; 4:1, 38; 6:1; 9:1). Finley, T. J. (2003). *Joel, Amos, Obadiah* (p. 258). Biblical Studies Press.

[4] Read Psalms 111:9. The title 'reverend' belongs to God. Note that no human in the Bible is called 'reverend.'

[5] http://www2.ed.gov/admins/finaid/accred/accreditation.html

[6] There are some fifteen different accrediting agencies recognized by the Secretary of Education. Many Christian institutions are member of the Transnational Association of Christian Colleges and Schools. Their manual can be found at: http://www.tracs.org/documents/2014AccreditationManual_003.pdf

[7] Tan, P. L. (1996). Encyclopedia of 7700 Illustrations: Signs of the Times. Garland, TX: Bible Communications, Inc.

[8] Finley, T. J. (2003). *Joel, Amos, Obadiah* (p. 100). Biblical Studies Press.

[9] Smith, S., & Cornwall, J. (1998). In *The exhaustive dictionary of Bible names* (p. 15). North Brunswick, NJ: Bridge-Logos.

[10] Finley, T. J. (2003). *Joel, Amos, Obadiah* (p. 100). Biblical Studies Press.

[11] Hubbard, D. A. (1989). *Joel and Amos: an Introduction and Commentary* (Vol. 25, pp. 143–144). Downers Grove, IL: InterVarsity Press.

[12] Spurgeon, C. H. (1868). *The Metropolitan Tabernacle Pulpit Sermons* (Vol. 14, pp. 14–15). London: Passmore & Alabaster.

[13] Morgan, R. J. (2000). Nelson's complete book of stories, illustrations, and quotes (electronic ed.). Nashville: Thomas Nelson Publishers.

[14] Would it be stunning to know that the word 'destiny' is not in the Bible? God never told us to 'discover our destiny.' He told us to "prove what *is* that good, and acceptable, and perfect, will of God" (Romans 12:2).

[15] Finley, T. J. (2003). *Joel, Amos, Obadiah* (p. 167). Biblical Studies Press.

[16] Hubbard, D. A. (1989). *Joel and Amos: an Introduction and Commentary* (Vol. 25, pp. 159–160). Downers Grove, IL: InterVarsity Press.

[17] Jeremiah 6:7; Jeremiah 20:8; Isaiah 60:18; Ezekiel 45:9; Habakkuk 1:3; Habakkuk 2:17

[18] See Exodus 21. The altar was a place of protection yet the law would not allow a murderer to be protected.

[19] Boice, J. M. (2002). The Minor Prophets: an expositional commentary (p. 186). Grand Rapids, MI: Baker Books.

[20] Hubbard, D. A. (1909). *Joel and Amos: an Introduction and Commentary* (Vol. 25, p. 172). Downers Grove, IL: InterVarsity Press.

[21] Baker, W., & Carpenter, E. E. (2003). The complete word study dictionary: Old Testament. Chattanooga, TN: AMG Publishers.

[22] http://www.christiantoday.com/article/joel.osteen.encourages.believers.to.trust.god.during.grief.trials.you.have.to.take.the.limits.off.of.god/47943.htm

[23] https://www.joycemeyer.org/articles/ea.aspx?article=this_is_only_a_test

[24] Larson, C. B., & Ten Elshof, P. (2008). *1001 illustrations that connect*. Grand Rapids, MI: Zondervan Publishing House.

[25] http://www.marshallparthenon.com/news/view.php/
682858/1970-Herd-member-Ed-Carter-returns-to-te

[26] Finley, T. J. (2003). *Joel, Amos, Obadiah* (p. 197). Biblical
Studies Press.

[27] Numbers 28:3; Deuteronomy 14:28-29

[28] Baker, W., & Carpenter, E. E. (2003). The complete word study
dictionary: Old Testament. Chattanooga, TN: AMG Publishers.

[29] Morgan, Rueben (1999). What the Lord Has Done In Me.
Hillsong Church. Sydney

[30] Boice, J. M. (2002). The Minor Prophets: an expositional
commentary (p. 205). Grand Rapids, MI: Baker Books.

[31] Boice, J. M. (2002). The Minor Prophets: an expositional
commentary (p. 205). Grand Rapids, MI: Baker Books.

[32] Hubbard, D. A. (1989). *Joel and Amos: an Introduction and
Commentary* (Vol. 25, pp. 203–204). Downers Grove, IL:
InterVarsity Press.

[33] http://www.nytimes.com/2013/04/09/science/when-weather-
changes-grasshopper-turns-locust.html?_r=1

[34] ibid.

[35] http://standupforthetruth.com/2011/03/signs-your-church-is-
going-seeker-sensitive/

[36] Baker, W., & Carpenter, E. E. (2003). The complete word study
dictionary: Old Testament (p. 449). Chattanooga, TN: AMG
Publishers.

[37] Stuart, D. (2002). *Hosea–Jonah* (Vol. 31, p. 385). Dallas:
Word, Incorporated

[38] Finley, T. J. (2003). *Joel, Amos, Obadiah* (p. 267). Biblical
Studies Press.

[39] Paxton, Gary (1975). He Was There All the Time. From the album: *The Astonishing, Outrageous, Amazing, Incredible, Unbelievable, Different World of Gary S. Paxton*

[40] http://www.gallup.com/poll/166613/four-report-attending-church-last-week.aspx

[41] http://en.wikipedia.org/wiki/List_of_sports_attendance_figures

[42] https://blog.faithlife.com/blog/2015/01/more-americans-read-the-bible-than-watch-the-superbowl/

[43] http://www.barna.org/congregations-articles/623-the-reading-habits-of-todays-pastors

[44] http://www.joelosteen.com/downloadables/pages/downloads/thisismybible_jom.pdf

[45] Pulpits are an interesting study. Historically, they were placed in the center of the stage because the preaching of the Bible was considered central. They were built to be very large so that the preacher would be hidden behind it. His personality was not important-the Word of God was. Pulpits stood for preaching Christ and preaching the Word. It is not an accident that one of the first 'changes' made in the modern church is the exchanging of a pulpit for a lectern

[46] See Romans 1:24-28.

[47] Stuart, D. (2002). *Hosea–Jonah* (Vol. 31, pp. 391–392). Dallas: Word, Incorporated.

[48] http://en.wikipedia.org/wiki/Carnival_of_Basel

[49] Galaxie Software. (2002). 10,000 Sermon Illustrations. Biblical Studies Press.

[50] Exodus 9:28; 1 Samuel 7:10; Isaiah 31:8

[51] http://www.boxingscene.com/thirty-years-later-weaver-vs-tate-remembered--26520

[52] Hubbard, D. A. (1989). *Joel and Amos: an Introduction and Commentary* (Vol. 25, p. 254). Downers Grove, IL: InterVarsity Press.

[53] https://www.gfamissions.org/missionary-biographies/crawford-dan-1870-1926.html

Books By Paul Schwanke

  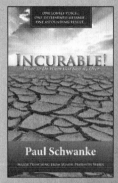

Major Messages from Minor Prophets Series

  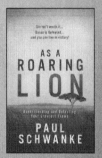 

Other Titles by Paul Schwanke

Evangelist Paul Schwanke

www.preachthebible.com

86265460R00069

Made in the USA
San Bernardino, CA
27 August 2018